U.S. China Policy and the Problem of Taiwan

U.S. CHINA POLICY AND THE PROBLEM OF TAIWAN

by William M. Bueler

Colorado Associated University Press
Boulder, Colorado

Colorado Associated University Press

Boulder, Colorado

Copyright © 1971 by Colorado Associated University Press, Boulder, Colorado 80302

International Standard Book Number: 87081-013-8

Library of Congress Catalog Card Number: 74-158666

Printed in the United States of America

Designed by David Comstock

Permission to quote excerpts from the following books is gratefully acknowledged:

Holbert N. Carroll, "The Congress and National Security Policy" in *The Congress and America's Future,* edited by David B. Truman, © 1965. Published by Prentice-Hall, Inc.

Dwight D. Eisenhower, *The White House Years: Mandate for Change, 1953-1956,* and *Waging Peace, 1956-1961.* Copyrights 1963 and 1965 by Doubleday and Company, Inc. Published in Great Britain by William Heinemann, Ltd.

Roger Hilsman, *To Move a Nation.* Copyright 1967 by Doubleday and Company, Inc. Excerpts reprinted by permission of Robert Lantz-Candida Donadio Literary Agency, Inc. Copyright 1964, 1967 by Roger Hilsman.

Arthur M. Schlesinger, Jr., *A Thousand Days.* Copyright 1965 by Houghton Mifflin Company.

William S. White, *The Professional: Lyndon B. Johnson.* Copyright 1964 by Houghton Mifflin Company.

Contents

Introduction

EVER SINCE THE NATIONALIST
Chinese government was forced to flee from the Chinese mainland
to Taiwan in December 1949, the United States has recognized it
not just as the government of Taiwan, but as the government of
the Republic of China. The policy continues today despite the fact
that since the 1950s no responsible U.S. policy maker has given
the Nationalists any realistic chance of recovering the China mainland. If the U.S. Government has for years believed that the
Nationalists would not regain the mainland, it has tacitly admitted
that the Nationalist government is not really qualified to call
itself the government of China. One can only conclude, therefore,
that U.S. support for the Nationalist regime as the legitimate
government of all China—support which continued at least until
1970—has long since failed to reflect U.S. policy makers' assumptions about the political realities of China and Taiwan.

The population of Taiwan is about 85 percent Taiwanese
and 15 percent Mainlander (i.e., Chinese who went to Taiwan
from the China mainland after 1945, and their children). The
Nationalist government is for all practical purposes the government of the Mainlanders; for instance, 98 percent of the members of the National Assembly are Mainlanders and 2 percent
are Taiwanese. Given the U.S. interest in keeping Taiwan out
of the hands of the Chinese Communists, the political interests
and aspirations of the Taiwanese might logically be expected to
have figured prominently in U.S. assumptions about Taiwan and

its government. The degree to which the Taiwanese have been taken into account in U.S. thinking and the accuracy of U.S. policy makers' assumptions about Taiwan is a major topic of this study.

The greatest single factor behind U.S. support for the Nationalists has probably been dislike for Peking. Thus, the question of U.S. policy toward Taiwan is closely related to that of assumptions about Communist China. The accuracy of these assumptions is the other main focus of this study.

Fundamentally, the United States faces four basic alternatives in regard to Taiwan: (1) to continue to recognize the Nationalist regime as the sole legitimate government of all China, (2) to support some form of "Two Chinas" arrangement in which the Nationalists would continue to exist as a "Free Chinese" alternative to Peking's Communist rule, (3) to allow Peking to take over the island, and (4) to work toward some solution that would recognize Peking as the government of mainland China and place the control of Taiwan in the hands of the Taiwanese people.

Such fundamental policy questions must be decided by the President of the United States. With this in mind, this book concentrates on the assumptions that have been held by the presidents and their top foreign policy advisors and is not simply a chronological record of policy decisions or a broad survey of American views about China policy and Taiwan.

The author assumes that the primary determinant of U.S. policy should be the U.S. national interest. In relation to Communist China and Taiwan our interest is to a very large extent a strategic one. The U.S. Government should be vitally concerned with the question of whether its strategic interests are best served by the present policy of support for the Mainlander-dominated Chinese Nationalist regime, or whether it would be more in the U.S. interest to encourage the development of a government on Taiwan which more genuinely represents the wishes of the Taiwanese majority. The latter would seem to be the case if it can be shown that in supporting the present government on Taiwan the United States is not only helping to assure the continued suppression of the genuine wishes of the people of

Taiwan but is also making U.S. relations with Communist China even more dangerous than they might otherwise be.

The 1970 United Nations vote on Chinese representation indicated to the U.S. Government that its traditional stand on this question probably cannot be continued for more than another year or two. The U.N. voting combined with the climate of world opinion has made it impossible to continue the fiction that the Nationalist Chinese government can represent China in the world community. By 1970 U.S. decision makers had been aware for at least a decade that the policy of support for the Nationalists as the legitimate government of China did not reflect the realities of the situation in China and Taiwan. But the events of 1970 for the first time caused the U.S. Government to realize that it must at an early date attempt to adjust its China policy to the realities of the Chinese situation. There is little reason to believe, given the apparent perceptions of U.S. policy makers today, that this adjustment would be unusually difficult —except for the exceedingly complex and difficult problem of Taiwan.

A fundamental re-examination of U.S. China policy has already begun. As it progresses, the Taiwan problem, including the internal political realities of Taiwan, will come under increasing scrutiny by concerned individuals both inside and outside of the Government. The Taiwan question is definitely a timely one, and it is hoped that this study can contribute in some small way to an understanding of it.

Truman
Administration

Before the end of 1949
it became clear to the Truman administration that the Nationalist
Chinese government of Chiang Kai-shek was going to be defeated
by the Communists. The conclusion that the administration drew
from this was that it would be in the interest of the United States
to move toward eventual recognition of the Communist victors.
Prior to the establishment of the Communist government in Peking
on October 1, 1949, however, there was little incentive for the
administration to directly confront the formidable pro-Chiang
sentiment in the United States and move toward recognition of
the Communists.

The only formal government in existence in China prior to
October 1949 was that of the Nationalists. Diplomatic practice and
international law fully justified delay in recognizing a new,
revolutionary regime until the dust had settled and the new regime
had firmly established effective control. Even more important
than considerations of international law, perhaps, was the U.S.
domestic political support for Chiang Kai-shek personally and for
his government. This support was well organized, highly vocal,
and ideologically committed.

Nevertheless, the establishment of the new government in
Peking, followed two months later by the flight of the remnants
of Chiang's government to Taiwan, gave the administration no
choice but to face the recognition issue. Twelve days after the
establishment of the Communist government, Secretary of State
Dean Acheson listed three conditions a new government must meet

before it would merit U.S. recognition: (1) it must exercise effective control, (2) it must recognize its international obligations, and (3) it must govern with the consent of the people.[1] Acheson indicated that he had the greatest doubts about point (2). His remarks implied that once Peking gave evidence that it would honor its international obligations, there would be no fundamental obstacle to the establishment of normal relations between the United States and Communist China.

After the flight of the Chiang government to Taiwan in December 1949, the administration faced two distinct but related problems: (1) what to do in regard to recognition of the new regime established on the mainland, and (2) what to do about Taiwan. The administration had up to this time firmly held that Taiwan was a part of China. It is likely that, in administration thinking in the period just after October 1, it was only a matter of time until the island would be incorporated into the new China.

Truman's thinking was made clear on January 5, 1950, when he issued a statement declaring that in conformity with the Cairo Declaration of December 1943 it was the U.S. view that Taiwan belonged to China. Stressing U.S. determination to avoid embroilment in Chinese internal affairs, the president stated: "The United States has no predatory designs on Formosa or any other Chinese territory. . . . The United States Government will not pursue a course which will lead to involvement in the civil conflict in China."[2] He said that the United States would not provide military aid or advice to the Nationalists on Taiwan in any effort to keep the island out of the hands of the Communists.

Since the administration had already concluded that without direct U.S. military intervention Taiwan could not be saved from Communist conquest,[3] Truman's remarks revealed quite clearly that the administration was prepared to allow Taiwan to fall to the Communists. The fundamental rationale behind this decision was obviously the desire to avoid intervention in what the administration considered the internal affairs of China. If, as the administration contended, Taiwan was Chinese, there could be nothing but trouble for the United States if it intervened to separate the island from the mainland government.

On the same day Secretary Acheson met with the press and

elaborated on the White House statement, adding even greater emphasis to the point that Taiwan legally belonged to China:

> The Chinese have administered Formosa for four years. Neither the United States nor any other ally ever questioned that authority and that occupation. When Formosa was made a province of China nobody raised any lawyers' doubts about that. That was regarded as in accordance with the commitments.[4]

Truman's statement had contained the sentence: "The United States has no desire to obtain special rights or privileges or to establish military bases [on Taiwan] at this time." This sentence raised the question, as Acheson asked rhetorically at his news conference, " . . . what does that phrase 'at this time' mean?" His explanation was:

> That phrase does not qualify or modify or weaken the fundamental policies stated in this declaration by the President in any respect. It is a recognition of the fact that, in the unlikely and unhappy event that our forces might be attacked in the Far East, the United States must be completely free to take whatever action in whatever area is necessary for its own security.[5]

In other words, while Acheson raised no doubts about the Chinese claim to Taiwan, he hinted that the administration would not hesitate to occupy this part of China if in a major war situation such occupation would be strategically advantageous for the United States. This pre-Korean War strategic contingency thinking facilitated the U.S. decision to neutralize the Taiwan Strait—the main purpose of which was to protect Taiwan from attack by Peking—just two days after the war broke out.

The question of U.S. relations with the Chiang government on Taiwan from 1949 to the present has been intertwined with that of U.S. recognition policy toward Communist China. Acheson's October 12 speech stipulating three conditions Peking must meet clearly indicated that at that time recognition was under consideration. However, there was neither then nor through the end of 1949 any indication that the administration sought the early establishment of diplomatic relations with Peking. As Acheson told the Senate Foreign Relations Committee on January 10, 1950, there was "no need for haste in recognizing" China's new leaders.[6]

On January 14, 1950, the Chinese seized the property of the American government in Peking. This action followed other incidents such as the arrest and beating of the American vice-consul by police in Shanghai in July 1949 and the jailing for a month of the consul general and some of his staff in Mukden in October. The United States considered Peking's January action the last straw and in response closed its diplomatic establishments in Communist China and withdrew its official personnel. On January 18 Acheson said at a press conference that the seizure of the Peking consulate made it clear that the Chinese were not interested in U.S. recognition.[7] The events of January 1950 brought an end to whatever momentum might have existed for recognition during the last three months of 1949.

There is no doubt that the hostile actions taken by the Chinese Communists against U.S. personnel and facilities justified a decision to withhold recognition until a satisfactory settlement and apologies had been made. For the administration, which was not eager to further stir the wrath of the domestic political opposition by rushing into recognition, these incidents provided a rationale for postponing recognition until some future, more politically auspicious, occasion. There is no indication that they convinced the administration that Communist China should never be recognized, but only that recognition must be delayed until the Chinese provided convincing evidence that they would observe accepted international practice.

From the Chinese point of view, their diplomatic transgressions were not without provocation. The Communists naturally resented U.S. aid to the Nationalists during the civil war, but they might have forgiven this eventually if the United States had not continued to back Chiang's regime after the Peking government was founded on October 1, 1949. In fact, of course, the United States continued to back Chiang even after the Nationalists were driven completely off the mainland in December 1949. It is obvious that the Chinese Communists would have served their purpose of winning recognition much better if they had been able to live with the U.S. policy for a while and had continued to treat American representatives with normal respect. This would clearly have been the means best designed to encourage the U.S. Government to deal with Peking on the basis of legitimacy and mutual respect.

Despite the reversal of the drift toward recognition, the administration did not alter its position that Taiwan belonged to China—and China now meant Communist China. On December 23, 1949, the State Department issued a policy paper stating that the fall of Taiwan to the Communists was expected and that in order to minimize the damage to U.S. prestige, U.S. missions abroad should play down the importance of Taiwan to U.S. interests.[8] The administration had decided that it had no choice but to make the best of a bad situation.

The establishment of the Peking regime soon raised the question of Peking's admission to the United Nations, and U.N. debates on this matter reached a head in January 1950. The U.S. position at that time was to vote against Peking's entry, but not to pressure other countries to vote the same way. On January 10, the U.S. representative in the Security Council, Ernest Gross, said that the United States would vote against a Soviet draft resolution to expel the Nationalists and admit the Communists, but the United States considered it a procedural rather than a substantive matter and would not veto it. The United States would "accept the decision of the Security Council on this matter when made by an affirmative vote of seven members."[9]

On January 13, the resolution was defeated by 6 votes to 3, with Norway and Britain abstaining. France voted with the majority, but Premier Bidault stated later that France had been on the verge of recognizing Peking and would certainly have done so in a short time if Peking had not recognized Ho Chi Minh's government on January 19.[10]

If France had switched its vote and if Norway and Britain had voted for Peking's entry, that would have totalled six of the seven votes needed; and if Egypt, as was expected, had soon recognized Peking, that would have made seven members of the

Council in favor of Peking. In the existing situation, in which it must have seemed quite apparent that Peking's admission was only a matter of time, Gross' statement indicating the United States would accept Peking's entry could have been expected to add further impetus to the drive to admit Peking. That it did not was due in part to Peking's recognition of Ho's regime, but even more to the Soviet Union's decision after the January 13 vote to absent itself from the Security Council for as long as China was represented by the "Kuomintang Reactionary Clique" rather than Peking.

This Soviet action greatly irritated other Security Council members and was self-defeating. It was probably the most important factor in preventing Peking's entry up to the time the Korean War began; after Korea, other factors came into play making it vastly more difficult for Peking to win admittance. Acheson reiterated in March 1950 that the United States would not use its veto to prevent Peking's entry,[11] and it appears that U.S. thinking on this remained unchanged up to the Korean War.

The Korean War brought about a fundamental change in U.S. China policy. It led to direct hostilities between the United States and Communist China, thereby increasing the animosity between the two countries; it can be said to have been Chiang Kai-shek's salvation. Prior to the outbreak of the war, despite highly vocal Republican demands to save Chiang, the Democratic administration had decided to make no serious effort to prevent the predicted Communist takeover of Taiwan; but one of the first moves made by Truman after the June 25 North Korean attack was the decision of June 27 to dispatch the Seventh Fleet to neutralize the Taiwan Strait. Although this was described by the administration as an "impartial neutralizing action" designed to prevent Nationalist attacks on the mainland as well as Communist attacks on Taiwan, the obvious primary purpose was to prevent, at least for the duration of the war, the Communist conquest of Taiwan.

Secretary Acheson acknowledged in a September 1950 television interview that the purpose in "neutralizing" the island was to "protect . . . the left flank of the whole United Nations position."[12] In terms of military strategy, for Taiwan to have come under Peking's domination would have released a large number of Chinese troops from the southeast coast of China who could have been moved to Manchuria to strengthen the Communist position near the Korean peninsula, but this strategic consideration was perhaps less important than the domestic political pressures for saving Taiwan. Before June 25 there had been much more concern about the possible loss of Taiwan than about South Korea, and to go to war to save the latter while abandoning the former would have made no sense from a domestic political viewpoint.

In January 1950 Acheson had defined the U.S. "defense perimeter" in such a way as to exclude both South Korea and Taiwan;[13] apparently he originally considered neither Korea nor Taiwan vital to U.S. interests. The same cannot be said for other elements of the U.S. polity, particularly the Republican senatorial opposition. These Republicans strongly demanded that the United States not let Taiwan fall, while there was no comparable group that was so concerned about Korea.[14]

With regard to Taiwan, the Republican demands built up gradually but steadily. In early November 1949, Senator H. Alexander Smith demanded that "under no condition" should the United States allow Taiwan to fall to the Communists; he suggested that the United States might want to exercise control over the island under a United Nations trusteeship.[15]

On December 30, Senator Knowland called for the dispatch of a U.S. military mission to Taiwan. Senator Taft, ex-President Hoover, and Representative Charles Eaton, the ranking Republican on the House Foreign Affairs Committee, were among others who at an early date showed an interest in a U.S. commitment to prevent the loss of Taiwan to the Communists.[16]

The Korean War and the ensuing decision to protect Taiwan brought not only a change in the military situation of the island, but also a fundamental shift in U.S. policy regarding its political and legal status. Prior to Korea, the administration had not publicly wavered from its view that Taiwan belonged to China, but on June 27, just two days after the North Korean attack, Truman announced that the status of the island in international law was undetermined: "The determination of the future status of Formosa must await the restoration of security in the Pacific, a peace settlement with Japan, or consideration by the United Nations."[17]

The administration's new position regarding Taiwan's status was in contradiction to the statements of Truman and Acheson in January, in which the administration had made clear that it considered the island's status settled—that is, that it belonged to China. Whatever good reasons the administration may have had for this shift—whether because of domestic political pressure or from a new conviction that Communist China did not have a valid legal claim to the island after all—the administration certainly had no reason to expect that the decision would be met with approval by the Chinese Communists. Chou En-lai made the Chinese position clear on June 28 with the following immediate reaction to Truman's statement of the previous day:

> I declare that Truman's statement of June 27 and the action of the American Navy constitute armed aggression against the territory of China. I declare that . . . the fact that Taiwan is part of China will remain unchanged forever.[18]

Truman probably did not intend to cut Taiwan permanently off from the mainland by his June 27 action. He appears to have recognized the nature of the problem that would arise with China if the United States forcibly prevented China from exercising sovereignty over Taiwan. On August 25 U.S. Ambassador to the United Nations Warren Austin listed several fundamental points about U.S. policy toward China and Taiwan, particularly with regard to the decision to neutralize the Taiwan Strait, and Truman states in his *Memoirs* that these points admirably summed up his thinking. The more significant items concerning Taiwan were:

> 3. The action of the United States was an impartial neutralizing action addressed both to the forces on Formosa and to those on the mainland. It was an action designed to keep the peace and was, therefore, in full accord with the spirit of the Charter of the United Nations. As President Truman has solidly declared, we have no designs on Formosa, and our action was not inspired by any desire to acquire a special position for the United States.

4. The action of the United States was expressly stated to be without prejudice to the future political settlement of the status of the island. The actual status of the island is that it is territory taken from Japan by the victory of the Allied forces in the Pacific. Like other such territories, its legal status cannot be fixed until there is international action to determine its future. The Chinese Government was asked by the Allies to take the surrender of the Japanese forces on the island. That is the reason the Chinese are there now.[19]

To Truman it may have seemed that the position as stated by Austin leaned over backward to point out that the United States had no aggressive aims in regard to China and that the United States was not foreclosing reversion to China as a possible ultimate solution for Taiwan, but to the Chinese Communists Austin's case was totally unacceptable. Their fundamental position was that the legal status of Taiwan had long since been finally settled. The Chinese felt, perhaps, as Americans would if the Russians occupied Hawaii and then tried to soothe American feelings by declaring that one possible ultimate solution for the state would be for it to revert to the United States. The implication that the United States would somehow play a part in determining who this Chinese island should belong to in the future was totally unacceptable to Peking.

In the light of the fact that the June 27 decision to protect Taiwan was at least partly in response to Republican opposition pressure, it is of interest to see what the thinking of leading Republican spokesmen was at that time. Prior to the outbreak of the war, no leading Republican argued that the remnants of the Chiang regime on Taiwan were qualified to be considered the legitimate government of all China; none betrayed doubts that Chiang had lost his position on the mainland for good. In fact, Republican senatorial leaders at that time thought more in terms of keeping Taiwan independent of Communist China than of seeing Taiwan used as a "Free Chinese" base for the eventual liberation of mainland China. In early January 1950, Senator Taft elaborated on the logic behind his demand for protection of Taiwan. Such a policy, he stated, did not commit us to backing the Nationalist Government in any prolonged war against the Chinese Communists. We can determine later whether we ever wish to recognize the Chinese Communists and what the ultimate disposition of Formosa shall be.[20]

Taft referred to Taiwan in these terms:

Here is a small area of the world, where, with no difficulty or expense, we could prevent the spread of communism to an island which might be of great strategic value and whose people desire to be independent.[21]

Senator H. Alexander Smith said on January 9 that what he had in mind for Taiwan was a "joint political authority and responsibility there between ourselves, the Nationalists, and the Formosan people." Smith also was against committing the United States "in an unlimited military way to the Nationalist cause."[22]

The interesting thing about these remarks is that at that time even those Republicans who were most eager for a U.S. commitment to defend Taiwan evinced no confidence about Chiang Kai-shek's ability to recover the mainland. They ignored Chiang's claim that he was the legitimate ruler of China and that he was only temporarily in Taiwan awaiting the opportune moment to launch a counterattack to wipe out the "Communist bandits." They likewise ignored the Chinese Communists' claim to Taiwan and, unlike the administration, seemed unaware that U.S. intervention would appear to Peking as illegal and totally unacceptable intervention in the internal affairs of China.

Taft and Smith were concerned primarily with the military advantage to the United States of keeping an island of possible strategic importance out of the hands of the Communist enemy. After the Korean War began, the strategic thinking of the Republican opposition changed drastically, and before long Taft and many of his colleagues were demanding military assistance to the Nationalists in an attempt to recover the mainland.[23]

The Korean War also brought about a tremendous change in the American public's views on China. Whereas a poll in 1949 showed 50 percent of the people in favor of the administration's decision to withhold further aid to the Nationalists, with only 20 percent disagreeing, a poll in 1951, at the height of the war, showed 58 percent in favor of providing assistance for a Nationalist attack on the mainland, with 24 percent opposed.[24]

The June 27 decision was followed in August by renewed arms shipments to the Nationalist regime. In January and February 1951 (two to three months after the Chinese Communists intervened in Korea) this aid became much more substantial, and in March 1951 the United States agreed to send a military assistance and advisory group to Taiwan. These steps signaled unqualified U.S. support for the Nationalist authorities as the rightful government of Taiwan, and, since that government never claimed to be just the government of Taiwan but rather the legitimate government of all China, this major commitment of U.S. aid implied that the United States was even willing to acquiesce in the Nationalist claim to legitimacy over all China.

In December 1950, British Prime Minister Attlee visited the the United States, primarily to talk about U.S. policy toward China and Taiwan. Truman's account of the conversation, as recounted in his *Memoirs*[25], reveals much of his administration's thinking about the problem of Taiwan. Attlee and his advisors were arguing for recognition of Peking and the reversion of Taiwan to China, while Truman and his advisors explained why the United States was unable and unwilling to make these concessions.

Truman was very critical of the Chiang Kai-shek regime, pointing out that Chiang showed little interest in improving conditions on Taiwan and was, instead, interested primarily in getting the United States involved in a war with Peking which would make it possible for him to get back to the mainland. Nevertheless, Acheson argued that despite the nature of Chiang's rule, the United States could not allow Taiwan to fall to the Communists, because the loss of Formosa would endanger Japan and the Philippines.[26] Secretary of Defense George Marshall remarked that the island was of no strategic use to the United States but would be very harmful if it fell into hostile hands.

Neither Marshall nor Acheson dwelled on the fact that this was a reversal of the administration's earlier position. (Acheson said on a later occasion that the Joint Chiefs of Staff had reviewed the Taiwan situation four times prior to the Korean War and decided each time that Taiwan was not essential to U.S. security.[27]) Undoubtedly the Korean War itself brought about this change in thinking.

More important than military considerations, perhaps, was Truman's acknowledgment of domestic political pressure on this issue. Truman pointed out that the United States in dealing with Chiang Kai-shek had to take account of the senatorial "clamor" on his behalf. The administration, Truman indicated, was limited in its freedom of maneuver regarding Far Eastern policy because the United States could not act abroad without solid backing at home. One of Truman's main arguments against Communist China's admission to the United Nations was that if this occurred there would be "terrible divisions" among the American people. Truman could not see what would be gained that would offset this "loss in public morale."[28]

At the conclusion of Attlee's visit, twenty-four Republican senators demanded in a resolution that Truman make known any "secret commitments" that might have been made to Attlee regarding possible recognition of Peking or abandonment of the Nationalists. Truman remarked sarcastically that these were the men who "thought a British prime minister was never to be trusted" while "Chiang Kai-shek could do no wrong."[29]

Although the Truman administration never seriously considered the possibility of promoting independence for Taiwan,[30] it was surely aware of reports that the Chiang regime had not distinguished itself on Taiwan and that it by no means enjoyed the whole-hearted support of the Taiwanese people. For instance, General Albert C. Wedemeyer, who led a presidential fact-finding mission to China in 1947 (and who later became a strongly anti-Communist supporter of "Free China"), reported:

> Our experience in Formosa is most enlightening. The administration of the former Governor Chen Yi has alienated the people from the Central Government. Many were forced to feel that conditions under autocratic rule [Japan's rule] were preferable.
> The Central Government lost a fine opportunity to indicate to the Chinese people and to the world at large its

capability to provide honest and efficient administration. They cannot attribute their failure to the activities of the Communists or of dissident elements. The people anticipated sincerely and enthusiastically deliverance from the Japanese yoke. However, Ch'en Yi and his henchmen ruthlessly, corruptly, and avariciously imposed their regime upon a happy and amenable population. The Army conducted themselves as conquerors. Secret police operated freely to intimidate and to facilitate exploitation by Central Government officials. . . .

There were indications that Formosans would be receptive toward United States guardianship and United Nations trusteeship. They fear that the Central Government contemplates bleeding their island to support the tottering and corrupt Nanking machine, and I think their fears well founded.[31]

Another critical report was that of a Central Intelligence Agency officer who expressed the view in 1949 that the Communists could take Taiwan without a full-scale invasion for two reasons: (1) the lack of discipline and low morale of the Nationalist troops, resulting from past defeats and poor leadership, and (2) the fact that Chiang's administration had earned him the "earnest hatred" of Taiwan's population.[32]

The "White Paper" (*United States Relations With China*) concluded:

The economic deterioration of the island and the administration of the mainland officials became so bad that on February 28, 1947, popular resentment erupted into a major rebellion. In the ensuing days the Government put down the revolt in a series of military actions which cost thousands of lives. Order was restored but the hatred of the mainland Chinese was increased.[33]

Given the available information indicating that the native Taiwanese were far from happy with Chiang's rule[34] and given the administration's conviction that Chiang's hope of regaining the mainland was negligible, if not non-existent, why did the administration not insist from the beginning that if Taiwan were not to revert to China it should become a de jure independent entity? The reason may have been that the prime goal of the administration was to avoid long-term involvement over Taiwan. Truman was probably less interested in assuring a non-Communist status for Taiwan than in arriving at an ultimate solution for Taiwan that would contribute to an eventual modus vivendi with China.

Since the administration realized that an independent Taiwan, especially under U.S. auspices, would have been totally unacceptable to the Chinese Communists, it probably reasoned that propping up the Chiang government until the end of the Korean War would do less damage to U.S.-Chinese relations over the long run than would permanently cutting off Taiwan from China. The course of giving aid to the Nationalists probably seemed to the administration to be the only one that would keep the island out of Peking's hands for the immediate future, without permanently fixing Chinese resentment toward the United States by forcibly removing Taiwan from Chinese suzerainty.

Another factor influencing the administration not to pursue a policy of independence for Taiwan was that after the Korean War began, and especially after the Chinese intervention in November 1950, the domestic political demand was no longer for merely keeping Taiwan out of Communist Chinese hands. Many Republicans and even some Democrats were now demanding that Chiang's regime be supported as a rival, non-Communist Chinese government. An independent, non-Chinese Taiwan would be inconsistent with a policy of using Taiwan as a "Free Chinese" base from which to work for the overthrow of communism in China.

After 1950 the policy of support for the Government of the Republic of China (GRC) on Taiwan became ever more firmly entrenched. By May 1951, Secretary of Defense Marshall was arguing that, if necessary, the United States should use its veto in the Security Council to keep Communist China out of the United Nations and that Taiwan "must never be allowed to come under control of a Communist government."[35] In June 1951, Acheson declared that Communist China should not be allowed to "shoot [its] way into the U.N."[36]

Perhaps the clearest signal that the administration had decided on full support for the GRC's claim to legitimacy as the government of all China came in an important May 1951 statement by Assistant Secretary of State for Far Eastern Affairs Dean Rusk. Rusk said:

> We do not recognize the authorities in Peiping for what they pretend to be. The Peiping regime may be a colonial Russian government—a Slavic Manchukuo on a larger scale. It is not the government of China. It does not pass the first test. It is not Chinese. . . . We recognize the National Government of the Republic of China, even though the territory under its control is severely restricted. We believe it more authentically represents the views of the great body of the people of China, particularly their historic demand for independence from foreign control. That government will continue to receive important aid and assistance from the United States.[37]

It is hard to imagine that either Truman or Acheson literally agreed with Rusk's views—which were completely contrary to those expressed by the president and the secretary of state before the Korean War—but Rusk's analysis represented the only logical rationale for the policy of continued support of the GRC as the government of China.

One can justifiably question whether Rusk himself (or his State Department colleagues) really believed the views he expressed. There is no real evidence that he did not. However, it should be recalled that the State Department in mid-1951 was under extreme pressure from the Congress to take a completely uncompromising stand against Communist China. Republican senators' cries of "appeasement" and accusations against Truman and Acheson for having "lost" China were heard almost daily.

The strongest attacks on the department came from Senator Joseph McCarthy. Although McCarthy unearthed no one in the department who could ever be convicted of having been a Communist agent, the pressures he generated led ultimately to the resignation or transfer from Chinese affairs of some twenty China specialists.[38] These included most of those whose on-the-spot reports (as published in the "White Paper") had been so critical of the faults of the Nationalist government that one could infer that their authors looked upon the unfolding Communist victory as something other than a moral and political disaster. The removal of those officers who had been most critical of the Chiang regime could not help but have discouraged those who remained from expressing views that were not strongly anti-Peking or pro-Chinese Nationalist.

Conclusion: The outbreak of the Korean War probably did not cause the Truman administration to change immediately its fundamental assumptions about the nature of the Communist or Nationalist regimes; the policy changes after June 1950 probably resulted from a combination of domestic political pressures and strategic considerations related to the Korean War and overall U.S. policy in the Far East. Neither Truman nor Acheson expressed any firm convictions about the future status of Taiwan. Instead, as Truman stated as early as June 27, once the Korean War began they considered Taiwan's legal status undefined. With regard to China, the administration's focus was on the mainland. Initially, at least, the interests of both the remnant Nationalist government on Taiwan and the native Taiwanese were considered relatively unimportant in comparison with the broader problem of U.S. relations with mainland China.

As to the degree to which the Taiwanese were entitled to be, or already considered themselves to be, a political entity separate from mainland China, the Truman administration was aware of this possibility but was not convinced that an independent Taiwan was a desirable and practicable alternative from the U.S. point of view. The promotion of independence for Taiwan would not have been easy. It would have required a full-scale commitment of American policy, and the goal would have been of questionable legal justification and of debatable benefit to long-term U.S. political interests. This uncertain goal would have been pursued in the face of stubborn opposition from the Chinese Communists, from Chiang's supporters in the United States, and from Chiang himself. Attainment of this goal would, in fact, have required the forcible elimination of the Chiang government. It is little wonder that with Korea, Indochina, and China itself in the forefront among the administration's concerns in Asia there was little inclination to strike out on a bold new course regarding Taiwan.

Eisenhower Administration

By November 1952 the partisan split on China had been partially closed. The issue of fixing blame for the "loss" of China had not been forgotten, but the differences that had existed before June 1950 in the two parties' official views concerning the nature of the Communist and Nationalist regimes had diminished considerably. The Democratic platform of 1952 revealed the extent to which that party had moved toward the Republican position: ". . . our military and economic assistance to the Nationalist Government of China on Formosa has strengthened that vital outpost of the free world and will be continued."[39]

This brief reference to China and Taiwan indicated a vast change in administration thinking over the preceding two years. It was diametrically opposed to the pre-Korean War views of President Truman and Secretary Acheson that Taiwan belonged to China, that "China" meant Communist China, and that it was in the U.S. interest to avoid getting involved in an effort to keep Taiwan out of Communist Chinese hands.

Despite the closing of the gap between the parties, the 1952 Republican platform, in addition to promising continued aid to the Nationalists, continued the partisan battle over China policy by blaming the Democratic administration for having "lost" China. The Democrats, the platform charged, had:

. . . required the National Government of China to surrender Manchuria with its strategic ports and railroads to the control of Communist Russia. They urged that Communists be taken into the Chinese Government and its military forces. And finally they denied the military aid that had been authorized by Congress and which was crucially needed if China were to be saved. Thus they substituted on our Pacific flank a murderous enemy for an ally and friend.[40]

With both parties now committed to protection of and assistance to the Nationalist regime on Taiwan, the newly elected Republican president—even if he had doubted the wisdom of a policy of non-recognition of Peking and support for the Nationalists—had very little room to maneuver. This is especially evident in view of the history of strong Republican friendship for Chiang's government and Republican criticism of the Democrats for not having done enough to save it.

Eisenhower's secretary of state, John Foster Dulles, forthrightly stated the fundamental assumptions that underlay the administration's China policy. On more than one occasion Dulles expressed the view that "international communism's rule of strict conformity is, in China as elsewhere, a passing and not a perpetual phase." He stated that it was the policy of the United States under his secretaryship "to do all that we can to contribute to that passing."[41]

This theme also found its way into official State Department statements of policy, for instance one dated August 11, 1958:

> The United States holds the view that communism's rule in China is not permanent and that it one day will pass. By withholding diplomatic recognition from Peiping it seeks to hasten that passing.[42]

This statement also said:

> . . . continued United States recognition and support of the Republic of China enables it to challenge the claim of the Chinese Communists to represent the Chinese people and keeps alive the hopes of those Chinese who are determined eventually to free their country of Communist rule.[43]

However, Dulles maintained consistently that the United States had no obligation to help the Nationalists retake the mainland, and when asked in February 1957 to comment on Senate Foreign Relations Committee Chairman Theodore Green's recommendation that the United States reconsider its non-recognition policy toward Peking, Dulles responded that although Green's advocacy had been "premature, to say the least . . . none of us are talking here in terms of eternity."[44]

In January 1958 Dulles remarked that the United States would recognize Communist China "any time it will serve the interests of the United States."[45] These comments imply that Dulles was less than absolutely certain that communism in China was merely a "passing phase." However, the general thrust of his statements from 1952 on indicates that he felt there was a very real chance that the Peking regime could eventually be replaced by a resurgent Nationalist China.

Prior to the Korean War, Dulles had taken a relatively moderate stand regarding Communist China. In early June 1950, with regard to a preliminary conference on a peace treaty with Japan, he proposed that both Chinas be present and that when they agreed they would together have one vote, while when they disagreed each would have a separate vote.[46] In his book *War or Peace,* published shortly before the Korean War began, Dulles said that if the Communist regime could govern "without serious domestic resistance" it should be admitted to the United Nations, although it "should not be recognized until it has been tested over a reasonable period of time."[47] At that time he was applying the traditional criteria for recognition, without treating China as a special case.

By 1952, however, Dulles had become attracted to the idea of "liberation" of China, rather than mere containment. In October 1952, he said:

Why should we assume that China is dead and done for so far as we are concerned? Why should we assume that what Soviet communism could do in China, we cannot undo? It will, no doubt, take several years of resourceful and imaginative effort to undo the disaster.[48]

Just three months later Dulles became secretary of state. One of the first changes in foreign policy made by the Eisenhower administration was the "unleashing" of Chiang Kai-shek, announced twelve days after the administration took office on January 20, 1953. Although it appeared to some people at the time that this "unleashing" was a direct outgrowth of the belief expressed by Dulles in October 1952 that the "disaster" could be "undone," the administration stated explicitly that the "unleashing" was not a prelude to a Nationalist "counterattack."

There is no indication that Dulles or Eisenhower ever considered the passing of the Peking regime to be imminent, nor that they ever seriously considered backing an early Nationalist bid to recover the mainland. As seen by Dulles, the recovery of the mainland, if it were to come at all, would presumably come at some indefinite time in the next decade or two. The 1953 "unleashing" was probably a reaction to Republican complaints that the U.S. neutralization of the Taiwan Strait constituted a protection of Communist China from Nationalist incursions rather than a reflection of the view that once "unleashed" Chiang would leap at the chance to land his forces on a mainland beachhead.

There is no indication that Dulles ever seriously considered the possiblity of U.S. support for Taiwan's self-determination or independence. Dulles does not appear to have been seriously concerned that the native Taiwanese might have a valid claim to a separate political identity of their own. Apparently, to Dulles the problem of Taiwan was exclusively a portion of the greater problem of China. He was unwilling to give up Taiwan, not because he was concerned about the political aspirations of the Taiwanese population, but because he hoped and perhaps believed that by keeping Taiwan ("Free China") out of the hands of Peking this island of presumed freedom would some day, in one way or other, have a beneficial effect on future developments in China.

By the latter part of his secretaryship Dulles came to believe that "Free China" should be a repository of the higher values of Chinese civilization, a custodian that would some day serve as a model for a newly enlightened China emerging from the dark ages of Communist tyranny. This was the case presented by Dulles in his conversations with Chiang Kai-shek in October 1958, at which time Dulles was attempting to persuade Chiang not to rely solely on military means to recover the mainland.[49]

Dulles felt that the proper policy toward the "Two Chinas" should be the same as toward the two Germanies and the two Koreas. Both Chancellor Adenauer and President Syngman Rhee had assured Dulles that for the greater purpose of world peace they would refrain from using military means to unify their countries under non-Communist regimes.[50] Provided peace could be maintained, Dulles believed, freedom would ultimately prevail in all these divided countries. It can be argued that the analogy with Germany and Korea was not wholly applicable to China and Taiwan. Dulles' plan assumed that what Chiang's regime represented on Taiwan would meet the test of time. If the "Free Chinese" way of life and government were expected eventually to win a free competition with Chinese Communism, it must have been assumed a priori that the "Free Chinese" government had the willing consent if not the active support of the governed on its own home ground. If, as is argued later, the great majority of the population of Taiwan would if given a free choice vote that government out of existence, there was a potential fallacy in Dulles' analogy.

In his memoirs (*The White House Years*)[51] President Eisenhower goes into some detail about policy toward China and Taiwan. His views were similar to those of Dulles, although he seems to have been somewhat less concerned about the future of China and Taiwan in moral and ideological terms while putting more emphasis on the strategic interests of the United States. Eisenhower's memoirs reveal almost no curiosity about the internal political realities of either Communist China or Taiwan. His assessment appears to have gone little farther than to recognize mainland China as part of the aggressive Communist world and Taiwan as part of the "Free World." In the light of this interpretation, the entire question of China policy was seen as part of the confrontation between the Communist world and the "Free World" led by the United States.

The offshore island crises of 1954 and 1958 were the most important problems Eisenhower faced with China and Taiwan.

To the extent that his memoirs touch on China policy, most of the space is devoted to these crises, and it is here that Eisenhower reveals in greatest depth his thinking about China and Taiwan. There is ample evidence that the Eisenhower administration was not happy that Chiang had placed so many of his troops on the offshore islands—especially on the Quemoys, the largest and closest to the mainland of the various island groups retained by the Nationalists after 1949.

Despite this displeasure and his conclusion that the islands were of little military value for the defense of Taiwan, during the 1954 crisis Eisenhower came to feel that these islands were so important that the United States should, if necessary, use nuclear weapons in their defense.

By what reasoning did this commitment come to be made for what was acknowledged to be virtually useless territory? The explanation lies in Eisenhower's assessment of the nature of the government on Taiwan. The reasoning ran as follows: Taiwan is indispensable to the defense of the "Free World"; since Taiwan's position in this defense depends on the morale of Chiang's army, this morale must be maintained at all costs; this morale depends on keeping alive the hope of returning to the mainland; the off-shore islands, especially Quemoy, symbolize the mainland recovery dream because they are so close to the mainland that the Communists and Nationalists can fire on each other and remind themselves and the world that they are still engaged in a civil war that must ultimately be decided by victory for one side or the other; if the islands were abandoned, the Nationalists in effect would be giving up their closest and most logical stepping stones to the mainland, thereby taking a major symbolic step away from returning to the mainland; this would destroy their morale and with it the Nationalist regime, which would be followed by the fall of Taiwan to Communist China. Therefore, Eisenhower concluded, the morale of the Nationalists must be maintained in order to assure the position of Taiwan in the island defense chain; since this morale depends on retention of the offshore islands, the defense of the offshore islands is consequently imperative.

Eisenhower's reasoning was clearly revealed during the first crisis in letters to his friend, British Prime Minister Winston

Churchill. The defensive nature of Eisenhower's arguments indicates that they were written in response to a challenge from Churchill. Eisenhower wrote:

> We believe that if international communism should penetrate the island barrier in the Western Pacific and thus be in a position to threaten the Philippines and Indonesia immediately and directly, all of us, including the free countries of Europe, would soon be in far worse trouble than we are now. Certainly that whole region would soon go.
>
> To defend Formosa the United States has been engaged in a long and costly program of arming and sustaining the Nationalist troops on that island. Those troops, however, and Chiang himself, are not content, now, to accept irrevocably and permanently, the status of "prisoners" on the island. They are held together by a conviction that some day they will go back to the mainland.
>
> As a consequence, their attitude toward Quemoy and the Matsus, which they deem the stepping stones between the two hostile regions, is that the surrender of those islands would destroy the reason for the existence of the Nationalist forces on Formosa. This, then, would mean the almost immediate conversion of that asset into a deadly danger, because the Communists would immediately take it over. . . .
>
> The morale of the Chinese Nationalists is important to us, so for the moment, and under existing conditions, we feel they must have certain assurances with respect to the offshore islands.[52]

In another letter to Churchill, Eisenhower wrote that while the United States (in Eisenhower's paraphrase of the letter in his memoirs) "could, for itself, assume an attitude of indifference to the fate of the islands, this would not ease, but rather would complicate, our problem, which was to assure the integrity of the island barrier in the Pacific." Eisenhower continues, quoting directly from the letter to Churchill:

> . . . We must not lose Chiang's army and we must maintain its strength, efficiency, and morale.

Concerning the possibility of a withdrawal from the offshore islands, he argued that

> the coercion we would have to exert to bring it about would so undermine the morale and the loyalty of the non-Communist forces on Formosa that they could not be counted on. Some, at least, might defect to the Communists or provide such a weak element in the defense of Formosa that an amphibious operation could give the Communists a strong foothold on Formosa.[53]

These passages indicate that in Eisenhower's thinking the the alternative to maintaining the hope of recovering the mainland was a collapse of morale among Chiang's forces. There was apparently no distinction in the president's mind between those factors which propped up the morale of Chiang and his followers who dreamed of returning to the mainland and those which affected the morale of the majority of the island's population. This lack of a distinction was made explicit in Eisenhower's instructions to Dulles for the latter's conversations with British Foreign Minister Anthony Eden. Eisenhower recalled in his memoirs:

> I suggested he tell Eden that we did not intend to blackmail Chiang into an evacuation of Quemoy and the Matsus as long as Chiang deemed their possession vital to the spirit and morale of the Formosan garrison and population.[54]

Eisenhower felt that the best way to defend the offshore islands and to avoid damage to the U.S. position in Asia would be to prevent a Communist attack in the first place. He was convinced that success at the negotiating table in Korea was the result of his implied threat that if the Communists did not agree to a cease-fire early in 1953 the United States might use atomic weapons to destroy their sanctuary in Manchuria.[55] Eisenhower undoubtedly believed that if the Chinese were similarly convinced that the United States would use its full power to defend the offshore islands they would not dare to attack.

Eisenhower did not want his hands tied to the extent that a Communist attack on Quemoy would automatically lead to atomic war; he wanted enough flexibility to withdraw under certain circumstances. On the other hand, he did want the authority to use whatever U.S. power might be needed to defend the islands. This desire led him in January 1955 to request Congress to pass the Formosa Resolution, which authorized the president to employ U.S. forces to defend Taiwan, the Pescadores, and "related positions and territories of that area now in friendly hands" (i.e., the offshore islands). The principle concerning the latter was that they would be defended if, in the opinion of the president, their defense was directly related to that of Taiwan. Since the U.S.-GRC Mutual Defense Treaty had been signed in December 1954 and was about to be ratified by the Senate, it was already quite clear that the United States would defend Taiwan and the Pescadores. In the debates on the Resolution there was no disagreement about this between senatorial supporters and opponents of the Resolution.

Everyone involved, including the public, understood that the only real issue was the extent of the American commitment to defend the offshore islands. This being the case, Eisenhower's conclusion in his memoirs concerning the effectiveness of the Resolution seems rather to miss the point. He says the Resolution, together with the mutual security treaty, "left no doubt of the United States' intention regarding Formosa and the Pescadores; in that region we would not be in the situation we had faced in the 1950 Korean crisis," and he doesn't mention the offshore islands at all.[56]

This omission might be the result of careless writing rather than unclear thinking, but it indicates that in Eisenhower's mind the fundamental question of what the United States should do to defend the offshore islands was surrounded by something less than precision. In fact, the Resolution (and the administration's overall policy in this crisis) did achieve the main purpose of deterring a Communist attack and thereby avoided a decision on whether or not to fight for Quemoy and Matsu. But the underlying problem of the existence of Nationalist-held islands within firing distance of the mainland remained as far from settlement as it had been before.

That the Formosa Resolution of January 1955 did not settle the issue permanently became clear in September 1958 when

Communist shelling of Quemoy initiated the second offshore islands crisis. By 1958 Chiang Kai-shek had increased his troops on Quemoy from about 50,000 to about 100,000, nearly a third of his effective ground forces.[57] The Eisenhower administration considered this increase unwise and firmly expressed the wish that Chiang had not made it. Dulles said at a news conference on September 30, 1958, "If there were a cease-fire in the area which seemed to be reasonably dependable, I think it would be foolish to keep these forces on these [offshore] islands. We thought it was rather foolish to put them there.[58]

Eisenhower acknowledged in his memoirs that Chiang "had helped complicate the problem" by building up his offshore strength, adding: "It seemed likely that his heavy deployment to these forward positions was designed to convince us that he was as committed to the defense of the offshore islands as he was to that of Formosa.[59] Thus, Eisenhower himself recognized that a primary purpose of Chiang was to put pressure on the United States. At the time of the crisis, Eisenhower had said Chiang's buildup was "not a good thing."[60] Secretary of Defense Neil McElroy, according to Eisenhower, felt that Chiang's insistence on keeping his forces on the offshore islands "was a reflection of his hope of promoting a fight between the United States and the Chinese Communists as a prelude to a Chinese Nationalist invasion of the mainland."[61]

If these views represented the thinking of the administration, it might have been expected to take toward Chiang an attitude of "He got himself into it, now let him get himself out of it." This was far from the case. The administration concluded that although Chiang had unwisely put himself and the United States into this predicament, the United States had no choice but to make a major commitment to defend Chiang's position. Eisenhower went out of his way to "allay the Generalissimo's [i.e., Chiang's] concern"[62] that the United States might have reduced its commitment.

The principle established by the Formosa Resolution, that the United States would defend the offshore islands if the islands were, in the opinion of the president, related to the defense of Taiwan and the Pescadores, was re-emphasized during the 1958 crisis. Eisenhower said at a news conference in late August that the Nationalists "have now deployed about a third of their forces to certain of these islands west of the Pescadores, and that makes a closer interlocking between the defense systems with Formosa than was the case before that."[63] Dulles said on September 4, "we have recognized that the securing and protecting of Quemoy and Matsu have increasingly become related to the defense of Taiwan."[64]

The Eisenhower administration was determined to avoid putting pressure on Chiang Kai-shek to abandon the offshore islands. As Admiral Arleigh Burke, Chief of Naval Operations, said on October 4, 1958:

> . . . it doesn't matter how we feel about giving up the offshore islands. It is the way President Chiang Kai-shek feels about it [that matters]. . . . We should not force him to give up the islands. . . . The principle is not for him to be forced—or for any other free nation to be forced—to take a position under pressure which they consider disadvantageous to them.[65]

Eisenhower's own thinking on the need to avoid forcing Chiang to change his ways had been made clear during the first offshore islands crisis in an April 1955 memorandum to Dulles, which said in part:

> To protect the prestige of Chiang and the morale of his forces, any alteration in military and political planning should obviously be developed under his leadership; above all, there must be no basis for public belief that the alterations came about through American intervention or coercion.[66]

Or, as Dulles said when asked by a congressman in March 1955 if there was any way the Nationalists could "withdraw from Quemoy and Matsu without disaster":

> Only . . . as a result of a decision made by Chiang Kai-shek on his own initiative that such a withdrawal would be good for Chinese Nationalist interests.[67]

In other words, the United States would not coerce Chiang to change his ways, even though the United States thought him wrong and even though Chiang's actions threatened to lead the United States into an unwanted war. Chiang's buildup on the offshore islands was undertaken, and is maintained to this day, with weapons and equipment provided by the United States. There is no indication that Eisenhower or subsequent administrations ever threatened a reduction of military aid in order to pressure Chiang into removing his forces from the offshore islands.

In the appendix of *Waging Peace*,[68] Eisenhower includes a remarkable memorandum worked out by himself and Dulles during the 1958 crisis. There is no doubt that this memorandum expressed his true thinking, since he explicitly states that he and Dulles went over it carefully to make sure that there was no disagreement between them.[69] The salient portions of the memorandum follow:

6) If Quemoy were lost either through assault or surrender, this would have a serious impact on the authority and military capability of the anti-Communist, pro-U.S., government on Formosa. It would be exposed to subversive and/or military action which would probably bring about a government which would eventually advocate union with Communist China and the elimination of U.S. positions on the island.

7) If the foregoing occurred, it would seriously jeopardize the anti-Communist barrier consisting of the insular and peninsular positions in the Western Pacific; e.g., Japan, Republic of Korea, Republic of China, Republic of the Philippines, Thailand, and Vietnam. Other governments in Southeast Asia such as those of Indonesia, Malaya, Cambodia, Laos and Burma would probably come fully under Communist influence. U.S. positions in this area, perhaps even Okinawa, would probably become untenable, or unusable, and Japan with its great industrial potential would probably fall within the Sino-Soviet orbit. These events would not happen all at once but would probably occur over a period of a few years. The consequences in the Far East would be even more far-reaching and catastrophic than those which followed when the United States allowed the Chinese mainland

to be taken over by the Chinese Communists, aided and abetted by the Soviet Union.

. . . .

11) Once we intervened to save the offshore islands, we could not abandon that result without unacceptable damage to the safety of the free world and our influence in it.

If accomplishment of this result required the use of nuclear weapons, there would be strong popular revulsion against the U.S. in most of the world. It would be particularly intense in Asia and particularly harmful to us in Japan.

If relatively small detonations were used with only air bursts, so that there would be no appreciable fallout or large civilian casualties, and if the matter were quickly closed, the revulsion might not be long-lived or entail consequences as far-reaching and permanent as though there had occurred the series of political reversals indicated in Point 7 above. It is not certain, however, that the operation could be thus limited in scope or time, and the risk of a more extensive use of nuclear weapons, and even a risk of general war, would have to be accepted.

The conclusion of this thinking is clearly stated by Eisenhower. "This modern possiblity that 'for want of a nail, a shoe was lost' had led to reaffirmation of the conclusion that Quemoy and Matsu were essential to American's security."[70] The logic behind this conclusion is based on Eisenhower's fundamental assumption that the Chiang regime must be maintained at all costs on Taiwan and that the continued effective existence of that regime depended on maintaining its morale by keeping open the prospect of a return to the mainland.

The line of assumptions tying the offshore islands' role in maintaining the morale of the "garrison and population" of Formosa to the security of the U.S. position in the Pacific apparently was never seriously questioned by Eisenhower or his advisors. During five years in Taiwan the author discussed the offshore islands with many Taiwanese and found that those who were willing to talk about the situation at all unanimously desired to see the offshore islands turned over to Peking. They considered them of no use whatever to Taiwan. The islands served only to keep alive Chiang's hope of returning to the mainland—a hope which all or virtually all Taiwanese consider a futile and foolish dream.

The Taiwanese felt that possession of the islands made eventual warfare between the GRC and Peking much more likely, and this would of course involve the native Taiwanese troops stationed on the islands. If, on the other hand, the GRC were to abandon the islands, the risk of war would be reduced: 100 miles of water between the mainland and Taiwan would put Taiwan out of reach of conventional Chinese Communist attack for the foreseeable future. The Taiwanese did agree with Eisenhower's reasoning on one point—that for the GRC to abandon the islands would be a serious blow to its morale and therefore its viability. Although Eisenhower hoped to avoid this eventuality, it was precisely what the Taiwanese wanted.

The Eisenhower administration's fundamental assumptions about the nature and role of "Free China" were intimately tied up with the assessment of the "other" China. Eisenhower, according to White House Special Assistant Sherman Adams, came into office with some doubts about the policy of non-recognition of Peking. In 1953, he refused to issue a statement desired by some Republican senators that the United States would never under any circumstances recognize Peking. He took this position because he wanted to keep open the possibility of recognition in case there later developed (in Adams' words) "a break between Russia and China or some other unexpected development [which] might make recognition of China a desirable strategic move in the best interests of the United States."[71] Later in his administration Eisenhower appears to have decided that any change in policy toward recognition of Communist China would be far in the future, and there was less said about the need to keep open the possibility of recognition.[72]

Eisenhower recalls an interesting incident during the visit of Premier Khrushchev to the United States in September 1959.[73] While talking at Camp David, Khrushchev said he had some comments to make about China and asked Eisenhower if he would like to discuss the subject. The President responded that he wasn't interested in discussing it because "Red China had put herself beyond the pale so far as the United States was concerned." Such a remark might seem strange to scholars or intelligence officers who would give their eye-teeth to hear a Russian premier's personal comments about China, but Eisenhower's response was consistent with his views about China, at least during the latter part of his administration. Peking had made itself the enemy of the United States and that was that. If the Chinese decided to completely change their hostile nature, the United States would be responsive, but until then there wasn't much point in talking about it.

Khrushchev said he had been asked by "someone" (Chinese? Russian?) to bring up the subject with Eisenhower, but Eisenhower apparently found the subject of China so unpleasant that he didn't bother to ask whom. Perhaps his refusal to discuss the issue with Khrushchev was a reflection of his view, expressed at an October 1958 news conference, that policy toward Communist China was "a very difficult thing even to study dispassionately and disinterestedly."[74]

Although Eisenhower may have had doubts all along about the real prospects for the GRC to recover the mainland, he indicated that he did at least want to keep this possibility open. An April 1955 memorandum to Dulles advocated "preparing and sustaining the bulk of [Chiang Kai-shek's] forces as a weapon of opportunity, ready to take advantage of any political, military or economic circumstance on the mainland that would give to an invasion a reasonable chance of success."[75] In other words, a GRC attempt to exploit by military means a situation of unrest on the mainland would not have been condemned by Eisenhower. This position is in contrast with that of Dulles in regard to the morality or legality of possible Communist Chinese use of force. Dulles stated on September 4, 1958, regarding the offshore islands crisis:

Neither Taiwan . . . nor the islands of Quemoy and Matsu have ever been under the authority of the Chinese Communists. . . . Any attempt on the part of the Chinese Communists now to seize these positions or any of them would be a crude violation of the principles upon which world order is based, namely, that no country should use armed force to seize new territory.[76]

The view that Communist Chinese use of armed force to take the offshore islands would be a "crude violation of the principles upon which world order is based" while GRC use of armed force to invade the mainland would be permissible is probably less an example of hypocrisy than simply a reflection of the view, as stated by Eisenhower to Khrushchev, that Communist China had put itself "beyond the pale." Peking, in Eisenhower's mind, was an outlaw regime and to apply to it the usual concepts of fair play or reciprocity was simply out of the question. John Foster Dulles' well-publicized refusal to shake hands with Chou En-lai at the Geneva Conference in 1954 was perhaps another reflection of this attitude.

It seems most unlikely that Eisenhower came into office with any well-formulated ideas about the two "Chinas" he had to deal with; he had had no close personal experience with China. His level of understanding could not reach beyond that of his major advisors and those groups to whose intellectual, political, and bureaucratic pressures he was subject—primarily the Republican party, the Congress, the State Department, and the military. All of these took a very hard line against Communist China and were strongly pro-Chinese Nationalist.

By 1952 most Republican congressmen had decided that the fall of China to the Communists had been primarily the fault of the preceding Democratic administration and not of Chiang himself. At the conclusion of the MacArthur hearings in August 1951, for instance, eight of the twelve Republican members of the Senate Foreign Relations and Armed Services joint committee which conducted the hearings issued a statement that concluded: "We have not been convinced that Chiang lost China for any reason other than that he did not receive sufficient support, both moral and material, from the United States"[77]—meaning, of course, the Democratic administration.

The tone of the Republican convention of 1952 regarding China policy was set by General MacArthur's keynote address which likewise put the blame for China's "loss" on the Democrats. As stated above, the Republican platform on which Eisenhower ran that year explicitly blamed the Truman administration for having brought about the communization of China. Given this climate of opinion within his own party, it would have taken monumental leadership on Eisenhower's part to pursue a policy of accommodation with Peking or to publicly refute the Chiang regime's claim to legitimacy as the government of China, even if that had been his desire.

Nor did the pressure from the Republican party cease with the election of a Republican administration. Eisenhower continued to be under intense pressure from his congressional party, headed by Majority Leader William Knowland, to take a firmer line of opposition to Peking and to provide greater help to the Nationalist regime on Taiwan. The president often found it necessary to attempt to temper the more extreme demands of the Senate Republicans.

In May 1953 Senator Dirksen proposed a rider to an appropriation bill for U.N. support, stating that the United States would terminate support of the United Nations if Peking were admitted. The rider passed the Appropriations Committee by 20-3, the supporters including all of the Republican members. It was only after direct negotiation with Eisenhower and Dulles that the leading Republicans on the committee agreed to accept a substitute amendment stating only that it was the "sense of Congress" that Red China should not be admitted to the United Nations;[78] this eventually passed both houses unanimously.

Essentially the same story was repeated the following year when Senator Knowland led a fight for a resolution declaring that the United States would withdraw from the United Nations if Peking were admitted. Once again, administration pressure toned this down to a "sense of Congress" declaration which was acceptable to the president.[79]

Eisenhower, in readily accepting the "sense of Congress" resolutions, made clear that he was by no means opposed to making a firm display of U.S. resolve to keep Peking out of the United Nations. But the important point about this congressional pressure is that even if the president had been in favor of a new approach, congressional resistance might have been too strong to overcome. Any sort of accommodation with Peking or significant lessening of support for the Chinese Nationalists would probably have required an open break with his party's congressional leaders.

In the 1940s, State Department observers in China contributed much of the highly critical information about Chiang Kai-shek's rule on the mainland which found its way into the "White Paper" (*United States Relations with China*). This document was obviously intended to illustrate to the public and the Congress the manifold failings of Nationalist rule on the mainland and thereby to justify the Truman administration's decision to avoid any further commitment to the Nationalists. It had the opposite effect on the Truman administration's critics, who interpreted it as a "whitewash" of the administration's "do-nothing" policy in China and claimed that it was proof that the administration, with Secretary Acheson and his State Department leading the way, had "lost" China through inaction and ineptitude.

The "White Paper" became grist for an intensified attack, led by Senator Joseph McCarthy, on the department. The effect of mccarthyism on the department's China specialists was to make it dangerous for them to be in favor of accommodation with Peking or too critical of the Chiang regime. In such a situation it was in the interest of those with doubts about the wisdom of U.S. policy to keep their doubts to themselves. By the beginning of the Eisenhower administration, the State Department appears to have become solidly committed to the policy of recognition of the Nationalists as the sole legitimate government of China and total non-accommodation with Peking.

The nature of some of the advice the State Department provided the Eisenhower administration is illustrated by the writings of Karl Rankin, who was the highest U.S. official in China and Taiwan from 1949 to 1959, the period in which China policy was fixed in its present mold. In Taiwan Rankin served as minister and charge d'affaires from mid-1950 to February 1953, at which time he was promoted to ambassador.

In his book *China Assignment* (1964)[80] Rankin quotes from many of his despatches to Washington. His approach to his reportorial task is indicated in the preface to his book,[81] where he points out that some of the excerpts from his despatches may "seem to support unduly the side of Nationalist China. This was done deliberately, for my pervading purpose was to assist those in Washington who shared my own sense of urgency about China. . . ."

After pointing out that the "shortcomings of the government of the Republic of China, now established on Taiwan, are an open book," Rankin says that he

felt no compulsion to add to these indictments. . . . On balance, the Republic of China was and remains a very great asset to the United States and the free world. . . . Criticizing [the Nationalists] needlessly only invites quotations out of context to the detriment of both American and Chinese interests. We cannot be "neutral" in any case.

In other words—and the entire text of the book bears this out—Rankin felt his purpose was not to remain objective in regard to Taiwan, but to convince doubters in Washington of what he believed was the necessity for the U.S. Government to support the GRC.

Rankin felt that one of his most important tasks was to help maintain the morale of the Nationalist regime, and this could be done only by keeping alive the hope of a return to the mainland. As he told a high-level conference of U.S. officials concerned with the Far East in 1956:

We must exert continuing efforts to bring about the reunification of China and Korea, in freedom. We should encourage our Asian friends in the belief that this can and will happen. We must keep hope alive and thereby sustain the morale so essential to surmounting the moral crisis facing the whole world today. . . .[82]

Rankin's book reveals no indication whatever that he questioned the right of the Nationalist regime to speak for all China and ultimately to return to the mainland. Nor is there any indication of doubt concerning that government's right to speak for the population of Taiwan. He seems to have accepted unquestioningly the Mainlander contention that the Taiwanese had no political aspirations of their own.

Rankin's book makes only three passing references to the 85 percent native Taiwanese majority, and there is no indication that during his nine years on Taiwan he ever held a meaningful discussion with a native Taiwanese. His only reference to the possibility of an independent Taiwan occurs on page 316: "Nor is there any real basis, and no desire in informed Chinese circles, for a permanent independent existence on the island of Taiwan." Rankin's "informed Chinese circles," of course, consisted of his Mainlander contacts who might stand to lose their official positions in an independent Taiwan.

Rankin's views about Mainlander-Taiwanese relations were echoed by his subordinates. One American scholar, Douglas Mendel, reports that during a visit to Taipei in 1957 he was told by the counsellor of the Embassy that " . . . we no longer make any distinction between Formosans and mainlanders—the gap has narrowed with education and prosperity and will disappear very soon."[83] (In 1961, Mendel brought up this remark in conversation with another State Department officer, who told him, " . . . we all say things like that in public, but most of us know better privately.")[84]

Another indication of embassy views was given to Mendel in 1961 (under Rankin's successor) when he arrived in Taiwan for a year on a Fulbright grant. "The Nationalist regime is very sensitive about certain issues," the Embassy cultural affairs officer warned, "and if you publish anything critical of your host government we may ask you to return home at your own expense."[85]

Rankin's immediate replacement as ambassador was Everitt Drumwright, a professional diplomat about whom Rankin wrote: "His Far Eastern background and known sympathy for Free China's cause made Drumwright an excellent choice."[86] With Dulles in the secretaryship, thoroughly pro-Chiang Walter Robertson as assistant secretary of state for Far Eastern affairs from 1953 to 1959,[87] and Rankin (or Drumwright) on the spot in Taipei, it is obvious that Eisenhower could have heard little from the State Department that would have caused him to question three fundamental assumptions: (1) Peking was not entitled to represent

China, (2) the Nationalist regime was essentially free and democratic, and (3) the native Taiwanese had no separate political aspirations that merited recognition.

As might be expected, the military has at times advocated an even more active policy of opposition to Peking and support for the Nationalists than has been pursued by Eisenhower's and succeeding administrations. One instance occurred during the offshore islands crisis of 1954, when three of the joint chiefs of staff (Radford, Carney, and Twining) "urged that the United States commit itself to defend the islands and help the Chinese Nationalists bomb the mainland." General Ridgway, army chief of staff, was the only member of the JCS who counselled otherwise.[88] The important thing here is not that the military has taken a militantly anti-communist position but that the military, for its own strategic interests, has been an additional pressure militating against any reconsideration of the nature of the Nationalist government on Taiwan.

Conclusion: The Eisenhower administration's policy toward China and Taiwan was of overriding importance in setting the course that has been followed into the 1970s. It is true that non-recognition of Peking and support for Chiang's refugee regime on Taiwan as the legitimate government of China began under Truman, but it appears that under Truman these policies were a reaction to the Korean War and were not conceived of as immutable fundamentals of China policy for decades to come. Almost certainly Truman and Acheson originally expected that, after the Korean War and a hoped-for stabilization of the Far Eastern situation, Peking would win its place as the legitimate government of China and some form of international action would be taken to settle the status of Taiwan in the light of that fact.

Under the Eisenhower administration a policy that had been undertaken by Truman as a temporary expedient became solidified as long-term, fundamental U.S. policy. Although both Eisenhower and Dulles indicated at times that they were not talking about eternity, they made it clear that they had no thought of altering this policy in the foreseeable future. By 1960 the policy of non-recognition of Peking and full support for the "Free Chinese" government on Taiwan had become firmly entrenched. It enjoyed such support from the State Department, the military, the Congress, both political parties, and the great majority of the American public that to have altered it would have required presidential leadership of heroic proportions. By 1960 the commitment to the GRC had become one of the firmest and most widely accepted commitments in American foreign policy, and no change was possible without a fundamental re-ordering of American priorities in the Far East.

Kennedy
Administration

THE KENNEDY ADMINISTRATION inherited a firmly established policy toward Communist China and Taiwan. Although Kennedy was never able to alter fundamentally that policy, he did question one of the assumptions upon which it was founded. Kennedy made it clear that he believed Communist China was here to stay and was not a "passing phase."

President Kennedy himself wrote very little about China. There exists nothing comparable to the memoirs of Truman and Eisenhower, which reveal much of their fundamental reasoning about the China/Taiwan problem as seen in retrospect. Available direct quotations from the president consist mainly of short passages from speeches which rarely had their central focus on China. We may assume that to the extent that these passages deal with China they do not do violence to his assumptions and the reasoning which underlay them; but broad statements about the state of the world rarely do more than reveal the most generalized conclusions about any single area.

Much more revealing than the president's own remarks are the writings of some of his advisors, particularly Roger Hilsman, who served as director of the Bureau of Intelligence and Research in the State Department from 1961 to March 1963, at which time he replaced Averell Harriman as assistant secretary of state for Far Eastern affairs. Hilsman was in an excellent position to assess the thinking of the administration about China. Kennedy's thinking as reported by Hilsman[89] is consistent with the president's own words and his views as reported by his biographers

Theodore C. Sorensen[90] and Arthur M. Schlesinger.[91]

Hilsman implies that President Kennedy had so many more pressing concerns during his presidency that he had little time to devote to China—clearly less than to Indochina, which was an immediate crisis area. Kennedy was interested in the China problem in long-range terms and sought ideas from his advisors and assistants, but he had neither the time nor the intimate knowledge to seriously attempt to reassess the fundamental assumptions urged upon him by the diplomatic, military, and intelligence bureaucracies he inherited.

Aside from some very early uninformed commentary about alleged Communist influence in the State Department having contributed to the loss of China to communism,[92] one of Kennedy's earliest public stands regarding China and Taiwan was taken during the senate debate over the 1955 Formosa Resolution, when he aligned himself with a group of twelve Democrats and one Republican who wanted explicitly to limit the U.S. commitment to the defence of Taiwan and the Pescadores—that is, in effect, to write off the offshore islands of Quemoy and Matsu.[93]

In the period preceding his election in 1960 Kennedy referred to the offshore islands on several occasions. During this period, shortly after the 1958 offshore islands crisis, the fate of these small outposts was much on the public mind. As in 1955, Kennedy favored a continuation of the Eisenhower administration's commitment "making clear our determination to defend [Taiwan]." However, concerning the offshore islands, he wrote in 1960, "The political and military reasons for defending Formosa do not apply to these two little islands [Quemoy and Matsu] just off the shore of Communist China." Our commitment there, he said, gives Peking the chance to put pressure on and take it off at will.[94]

On another occasion Kennedy stressed that control over the issue of war and peace should be in our hands but that in the existing situation there was danger of our being dragged into war over Quemoy and Matsu by the actions of Chiang Kai-shek, and, he said, the United States would have no allies in a war over these islands.[95]

Kennedy undoubtedly felt at the time that his pre-election position on the offshore islands was realistic, but after his inauguration the political situation he faced caused him to alter his original position. When the Communists began to build up their forces opposite Quemoy in 1962, Kennedy went out of his way to point out that "our policy . . . remains just what it has been on this matter since 1955"[96]—that is, since the 1955 Formosa Resolution. This could only have been an implied warning to Peking that the United States might well defend the islands against a Communist attack.

What brought about this change in the president's thinking? Undoubtedly Kennedy was subjected to substantial pressures from both the Chinese Nationalists and from within the U.S. Government to avoid changing established policy on this question. The situation he faced as president was this: if he was not willing to assist in the defense of the offshore islands, he would be responsible for forcing Chiang Kai-shek to make one of two choices: (1) to pull back to Taiwan, or (2) to stand and fight—and probably lose. Either choice would be a disastrous blow to Chiang's dream of recovering the mainland.

If Chiang were forced to retreat 100 miles across the Taiwan Strait, the trend toward a separate existence for Taiwan would be given a great boost. Once the world and the Taiwanese saw Chiang retreat from the offshore islands the handwriting on the wall would be very clear—Chiang would not be going back. Since the sole raison d'etre of the GRC is the recovery of the mainland,[97] the admission of the impossibility of the dream that would be signalled by the abandonment of the offshore islands—the "stepping stones" for recovering the mainland—would be an almost mortal blow to the GRC's prestige, both internationally and internally.

In other words, for Kennedy to have made clear that the United States would not defend the offshore islands would have been a serious and possibly fatal blow to the GRC. His decision concerning the offshore islands could not be isolated from his and the U.S. Government's fundamental assumptions concerning Taiwan and the GRC: if the continued existence of a "Free Chinese" government able to challenge Peking's right to speak for China was vital to the U.S. national interest, the retention of the offshore islands in GRC hands was also in the U.S. interest.

Concerning Communist China, Kennedy accepted the belief that in all probability it is here to stay. Although he did not dwell publicly on this point at the expense of the prestige of our GRC ally, his remarks clearly implied Peking's permanence. He went so far as to inform the GRC privately that U.S. policy was now based on this assumption,[98] and he made known his belief that in the foreseeable future Communist China would be a growing problem. Before his death he approved Hilsman's December 1963 speech publicly proclaiming that the new assumption that Communist China was here to stay had replaced the previous administration's assumption that it was a "passing phase."

Nevertheless, Kennedy refused to withdraw U.S. support from the GRC, not only as the government of Taiwan, but also as the legitimate government of all China. He did not deviate from the Eisenhower administration's policy toward Chinese representation in the United Nations. According to the joint statement issued at the time of the late GRC Vice President Ch'en Ch'eng's visit to the United States in August 1961:

The President reiterated firm United States support for continued representation of the Republic of China in the United Nations, of which she is a founding member. He also reaffirmed the U.S. determination to continue to oppose admission of the Chinese Communist regime to the United Nations.[99]

In April 1961, following talks with British Prime Minister Macmillan, Kennedy had told a news conference:

I made it very clear [to Macmillan] that the United States was going to continue to meet its commitments to the people on Formosa—the government on Formosa. . . . I want to take this opportunity to emphasize that the United States supports the [GRC] in its membership in the United Nations. . . . The United States . . . continues to be opposed under present conditions to the admission of Red China [to the United Nations].[100]

Hilsman states that in 1961 the administration was "fighting desperately" to maintain the GRC's seat in the United Nations.[101] But, one might ask, why was the GRC's presence in the China seat so greatly in the U.S. interest if the notion that the GRC would recover the mainland was, to use Hilsman's word, a "myth"?[102] The only answer evident from Hilsman is that the United States was so committed on this issue that to lose would have been a blow to our prestige and would have serious domestic ramifications. In Hilsman's words:

> Such a resounding defeat of a long-standing American policy would obviously be damaging internationally. And the repercussions domestically, in the general public and in Congress, would be horrendous.[103]

Perhaps the true state of President Kennedy's thinking was indicated in his 1961 remarks to U. N. Ambassador Adlai Stevenson about Stevenson's impending efforts on behalf of the U. S. position on the China representation question:

> "You have the hardest thing in the world to sell. It really doesn't make any sense—the idea that Taiwan represents China. But, if we lost this fight, if Red China comes into the U.N. during our first year in town . . . they'll run us both out. We have to lick them this year. We'll take our chances next year. It will be an election year; but we can delay the admission of Red China till after the elections. . . ."
>
> Stevenson asked, "Do you mean to keep them out permanently or for a year?" Kennedy said, "At least for a year. . . ."[104]

In 1962 the Communists began a major buildup of their forces opposite Quemoy. This created perhaps the closest thing to a direct confrontation with China that the Kennedy administration faced. The first task was to determine the aim of the buildup. According to Hilsman, three theories were held by various members of the administration as possible explanations of the buildup: (1) it was defensive, designed to either deter or defend against a U.S.-supported Nationalist assault, (2) Peking was planning a repeat of the 1958 bombardment of Quemoy, (3) the

Communists were planning an attack not just on the offshore islands, but also on Taiwan.

According to Hilsman, the intelligence community, "possibly influenced by [CIA Director] John McCone's somewhat apocalyptic view that sooner or later a showdown with the Chinese Communists was inevitable," argued in favor of (3).[105] At a high-level meeting in the White House in June, Secretary of Defense Robert McNamara "spoke not only with passion against (3) . . . but with contempt." McNamara "thoroughly demolished" the notion that the Communists were planning an attack by demonstrating that their available landing equipment was inadequate for an assault even on the offshore islands, much less on Taiwan.[106]

The Chinese Communist buildup coincided with an intense GRC propaganda campaign about the long-heralded "counterattack".[107] In fact, the first of the three alternative theories mentioned above implied that the Communists, quite the opposite from planning an invasion, were reacting defensively to the Nationalist campaign. Hilsman says that this interpretation gradually gained weight in administration thinking. In order to make sure that Peking did not believe the United States was behind the Nationalist campaign, the U.S. ambassador in Warsaw was instructed to assure the Chinese ambassador on June 26 that there would be no U.S. support for "any Nationalist attempt to invade the mainland."[108]

Chiang Kai-shek had never ceased his call for a "counterattack" to deliver the mainland from the clutches of the "Communist bandits." Whether or not anyone believed his oft-repeated call, the maintenance of the entire political structure of the GRC was, and is, justified solely by this goal. As Chiang himself has said, "Either we exist to return to the mainland or we have no existence worth mentioning."[109] In early 1962, Chiang had said:

> Either subjectively or objectively we can no longer vacillate or hesitate to perform our duty to deliver our people, our nation and the whole world from catastrophe. . . . The situation, both at home and abroad, is such that we can no longer passively wait and see if something will happen.[110]

What Chiang was saying just prior to the Communist buildup, in other words, was that the GRC should take the initiative to deliver the China mainland from the Communists.

Chiang himself appears to see mainland recovery as a mission of personal vindication as much as a historical necessity or inevitability. In addressing the National Assembly in 1960 he personally assumed the blame for the failure of the GRC to recover the mainland, saying: "So great is my fault that I wish sincerely to surrender myself to you for punishment."[111] He remarked on the occasion of his re-election to a fourth term as president, in 1966:

> As I am approaching 80, I would prefer retirement and return to private life. But I have been encouraged by the constant thought that I should redeem myself for what I have thus far failed to do for our nation. I feel my obligation unfulfilled so long as the Chinese mainland is not recovered.[112]

These expressions of contrition indicate something of the lamentable state of the man and the dream.

The Great Leap Forward which began on the mainland in 1958 did unquestionably bring serious difficulties to the Chinese people on the mainland, and this clearly generated dissatisfaction if not outright disaffection. Peking's difficulties gave new lease on life to the Chiang dream; after 1959 GRC expressions of confidence that the time had finally come for the counterattack became increasingly more frequent. This rhetoric reached a peak in the GRC's 1962 campaign to persuade the United States to back an assault.

At the height of this campaign, Hilsman personally went to Taipei for talks with Chiang Ching-kuo ("CCK"), Chiang Kai-shek's son and heir apparent. CCK made an impressive case for launching an attack on the mainland. As much as Hilsman "would have liked to believe that the Chinese regime was about to topple," however, CCK failed to convince him that an attack should be launched. Yet Hilsman concluded that although the prospects were extremely remote "there was always some possibility that new evidence would support the notion that the mass of the people would revolt and no one wanted to overlook such a possibility."[113]

Clearly, Hilsman never believed that the GRC had a significant chance of recovering the mainland. Nevertheless, he and the administration as a whole could not pull themselves away entirely from the temptation to examine reports of mainland dissent to see if there might be enough of it to threaten the stability of the Communist regime. In other words, although the administration leaders never seriously considered backing an effort to topple Peking, they continued to feel that such an unlikely development would have been desirable. The administration was reluctant to close off irrevocably all possibility of seeing the GRC take advantage of possible future chaos on the mainland. Hilsman stated:

> For the Kennedy administration, the dilemma was clear. If the United States encouraged Chiang, and it turned out that the Communist regime was not ready to topple, it would be the Bay of Pigs all over again, only much, much worse. . . . On the other hand, if the Communist regime was really ready to topple and the United States failed to support the Nationalists, the Democrats would stand accused of being the only party in history that lost China twice. . . .[114]

In regard to the 1962 events, the administration finally decided to urge the GRC to acquire more intelligence; in Hilsman's words, ". . . it would be better for the Nationalists to reach that conclusion [that the mainland was not ripe for rebellion] themselves on the basis of the evidence than for the United States to try to force it on them."[115] Theodore Sorensen, in describing the events at this time, says that President Kennedy

> had no confidence in Chiang's ability to regain control of the mainland, even with American assistance. . . . Without giving Chiang the kind of flat rejection the Generalissimo might exploit politically, he politely informed him that the time was not ripe and that unlimited American backing would not be forthcoming.[116]

It can be argued that the fear that the GRC might "exploit politically" a "flat rejection" totally misses the point. It can be argued that it was precisely the sort of temporizing described by Sorensen that the GRC could exploit politically because it did not explicitly wipe out the futile hope of recovering the mainland. International acceptance of the GRC's claimed status as a legal government of China depends almost entirely on U.S. support.[117] If the United States explicitly denied that the GRC had the right to recover the mainland, it would in effect be saying that the GRC was not really the government of China. And if the GRC, with its Mainlander monopoly of power, ceased to be the government of China, it would have no right to govern Taiwan—as GRC supporters readily admit. Therefore, U.S. unwillingness to flatly reject the GRC's claimed right to recover the mainland has been indispensable to continued GRC control of Taiwan. Thus, it can be argued in exact contradiction of Sorensen's remark, it was precisely the refusal of the United States to give a "flat rejection" that the GRC was able to "exploit politically."

Hilsman says, as quoted above, that it would be better for the Nationalists to "reach that conclusion [i.e., that the mainland Chinese were not about to rebel] themselves on the basis of the evidence. . . ." Hilsman implies here that the GRC wanted to take action only because they had insufficient information to convince them it would be unwise. This also can be viewed as a fundamental misinterpretation of GRC aims—that in fact it was less the GRC's purpose to acquire an accurate understanding of the stiutation on the mainland than to convince the United States that it should decide to back a GRC effort to recover the mainland.

That awareness of this possible interpretation was not absent from administration thinking was indicated by Hilsman:

> Cynics felt that what was really intended in the idea of landing a division or two on the mainland was not so much to trigger a revolt as to trigger American intervention—to create a situation in which the United States would be forced to come to the aid of beleaguered Nationalist troops on a mainland beachhead and so precipitate a major war between the United States and Communist China that would put the Nationalists back in power.[118]

President Kennedy and his advisors appear to have made little or no public comment on the question of whether or not the native Taiwanese population might have legitimate aspirations of their own in conflict with those of the Mainlander regime. On one occasion, in response to a question at a news conference, Kennedy remarked, "Quite obviously, [it is] the desire . . . of the people of Formosa that they be returned [to the Chinese mainland]."[119] It is doubtful that this isolated comment was made on the basis of long study of the question with the conclusion reached that the native Taiwanese were eager to "return" to the mainland. By "people" Kennedy undoubtedly referred to those whose views had been reported to him through official channels, namely the people who made up the GRC—who were Mainlanders and who did indeed desire to return to the mainland.

The administration was not unaware of tension between the Taiwanese and the Mainlanders. Hilsman comments: "Politically, reports of Chiang Kai-shek's continued dictatorship and the oppression of Taiwanese by the 'Mainlanders' made the Nationalists no asset to the United States."[120] Yet this is the only meaningful reference in his book to the internal political tensions on Taiwan. Hilsman does not elaborate on the possible significance for U.S. policy if the Chiang regime was, as reported, an oppressive dictatorship rather than an entity which merited the appellation "Free China."

One of the most interesting parts of Hilsman's account concerns the political pressures, particularly from Congress, that operated on the administration in regard to policy toward China and Taiwan. One view of congressional influence on China policy has been given by Holbert N. Carroll:

Only in the case of Communist China has the Congress played a major role over a long period of time to confine narrowly the President's means of maneuver. In the late 1940s and early 1950s the Congress served as the forum for developing and expressing the version of why China went Communist that was to permeate the public most deeply. Beginning in the early 1950s the Congress went on record each year, often more than once and usually with no dissenting voices, to oppose the seating of Communist China in the United Nations. . . . By these resolution, by amendments to various laws, and in other ways, the Congress constructed formidable walls for any President, if so inclined, to breach. [121]

The pressure from Congress was illustrated during the Kennedy administration in relation to the Mongolian recognition question in 1961. According to Hilsman, once it became known that the administration was considering recognition, congressional supporters of the China lobby, including members of both parties, "quietly let it be known" that, if the administration went ahead with its plan, they would "destroy Kennedy's foreign aid program with crippling amendments."[122] Republican Senator Kenneth Keating concluded ominously that the Mongolian move must be an opening wedge for getting Communist China into the United Nations.[123] Hilsman makes it quite clear that although Kennedy himself favored the Mongolian recognition plan, he backed down primarily because of the hostile reaction of Congress.[124]

In 1961 the administration became convinced that the moratorium on discussion of Communist China's entry into the United Nations could no longer be maintained, and it began to search for some other way to keep Peking out. Finally it hit upon the "important question" formula as a new strategy to promote this aim, reasoning that it would be some time before two-thirds of the U.N. members would vote to admit the Communists at the expense of expelling the GRC. The mere thought that the United States was now willing to discuss the question of Peking's entry, however, raised a storm in Congress. In July, when Senator Dirksen proposed a resolution opposing Peking's entry, Senator Mansfield questioned the need for another such resolution since there had been one every year since the early 1950s and all of them were still good. Dirksen responded that another resolution was indeed needed in order to "mobilize public opinion" because the administration was playing "Russian roulette" with China policy. [125] Dirksen's resolution passed without a dissenting vote.

The administration was able to go through with its plan to use the "important question" formula because anti-Peking senators finally realized it was probably necessary if Communist China were to be kept out of the United Nations. The thought that the administration might consider even a slight change in China policy, however, had raised congressional hackles. The administration was reminded—if it needed reminding—that any fundamental shift from the policy of non-accommodation with Peking (with its corollary of full support for the GRC) might well cause a serious break between Congress and the administration.

Conclusion: The Kennedy administration formally announced that it had altered the assumption that communism in China was a passing phase. This position was important in relation to long-range aims but had little impact on short-term policy toward China and Taiwan. Policy toward Taiwan was still based on the assumption that continued support for the Nationalist regime was in the U.S. interest. Presumably a major reason for this was the strategic interest in retaining Taiwan as part of the Pacific island defense chain, but Kennedy does not appear to have dwelt on this to the extent that Eisenhower did.[126]

There is little indication that the Kennedy administration spent much time worrying about Taiwan as such. With Vietnam, Laos and China itself in the forefront of Asian concerns, the internal political situation on Taiwan remained on the "back burner," as they say in bureaucrateze. The basic thinking behind the U.S. commitment to the GRC had been done by the previous administration; Kennedy inherited the situation, the policy, and the assumptions. At least some members of his administration were aware that "Free China" was no haven of freedom for the native Taiwanese, but there is no indication that this awareness led them to search seriously for a new policy which would put more emphasis on the aspirations of the majority group on Taiwan.

The domestic political pressures on Kennedy were essentially the same as those faced by Eisenhower. They all pushed him in one direction—anti-Peking and pro-Taipei. There was little congressional or public pressure either to take a more compromising line against Peking or to work for the interests of the Taiwanese as opposed to those of the GRC on Taiwan. The pressures Kennedy faced would have made it extremely difficult for him to adopt a new policy toward China and Taiwan even if he had been intellectually convinced that a basic change in the direction of U.S. policy was necessary during his term of office.

Kennedy did believe that the United States would eventually have to reach an accommodation with Peking; his personal inclination would probably have been to take such a step as soon as politically feasible—the sooner the better. Both Sorensen and Hilsman report that Kennedy planned to attack the China problem with greater vigor during his "second administration."[127] But the fact that he believed fundamental policy changes could be put off until after his first term indicates that in his view the China problem was not so urgent that major steps needed to be taken to solve it irrespective of the political pressures under which he had to operate.

Johnson Administration

THE JOHNSON ADMINISTRATION inherited the China policy handed down from Eisenhower, modified by Kennedy's somewhat revised assumptions about Chinese reality. Johnson apparently made little further searching inquiry into the assumptions, nor did he significantly alter the policy. During the last three years of the administration the Vietnam war so dominated the Asian scene that a serious reconsideration of the fundamental direction of China policy was for all intents and purposes out of the question. Prior to his presidency, Johnson had never even attempted to be an authoritative spokesman on Far Eastern policy. His views about China and Taiwan, even more than those of his predecessors, were the product of the views of his advisors and of the political pressures of the times rather than the result of a long-time interest in the China problem.

Johnson's public references to China and Taiwan stressed the view that any change in the existing hostility between the United States and Communist China depended on a change of heart on the part of the latter; he strongly reaffirmed existing commitments to the GRC. In a speech in April 1964, for instance, he said:

> . . . so long as the Communist Chinese pursue conflict and preach violence, there can be and will be no easing of relationships. There are some who prophesy that these policies will change. But America must base her acts on present realities and not on future hopes. It is not we who must re-examine

our view of China, it is the Chinese Communists who must re-examine their view of the world.

Nor can anyone doubt our unalterable commitment to the defense and liberty of free China. . . .[128]

The commitment to the GRC meant continued public support for its claim to be the legitimate government of all China, for to openly deny that claim would have meant to remove the raison d'etre of that regime.

Johnson often spoke of the desire for more contact with Communist China. However, it is a central thesis of this book that Peking means it when she says she does not want an improvement in relations with the United States as long as the United States recognizes a rival Chinese regime on Taiwan. If this is true, it is not difficult to see why Johnson's tentative probings in this direction did not result in an improvement in Sino-Amercan relations. In Peking's view, the Johnson administration's efforts to increase friendly contact with Peking while continuing its "armed occupation" of "China's territory of Taiwan" were, to use Peking's words, a "sham," a "trick," and a "conspiracy."[129]

In 1961, Johnson, as vice-president, made a trip to the Far East. After a brief visit to Taiwan he concluded in a memorandum to President Kennedy:

The Republic of China on Taiwan was a pleasant surprise to me. I had long been aware of the criticisms against Chiang Kai-shek and his government and cognizant of the deep emotional American feelings in some quarters against him. I know these feelings influence our U.S. policy. Whatever the cause, a progressive attitude is emerging there. Our conversations with Chiang and Mme. Chiang were dominated by discussions of measures of social progress to my gratified surprise. . . .[130]

If this first-hand impression represented the views Johnson brought into the presidency concerning the internal situation in Taiwan, it is unlikely that, given the other problems he faced as president, occasional reports of GRC suppression of Taiwanese opposition would have had a very great impact on his thinking.

Johnson's own views on policy toward China and Taiwan were not spelled out as explicitly as those of Secretary of State Dean Rusk in his numerous references to the subject. The burden of Rusk's message was that if China would "renounce the use of force" against its neighbors, particularly Taiwan, she would find the United States responsive. The real problem here was Taiwan. In remarks to the Far East and Pacific Subcommittee of the House Foreign Affairs Committee, on March 16, 1966, Rusk outlined ten elements for a sound future China policy. The third point was:

> We must honor our commitments to the Republic of China and to the people on Taiwan, who do not want to live under communism. We will continue to assist in their defense and to try to persuade the Chinese Communists to join with us in renouncing the use of force in the area of Taiwan.

The fourth point was that the United States would continue its efforts to "prevent the expulsion of the Republic of China from the United Nations," and to oppose the entry of Communist China as long as it "follows its present course."[131]

Rusk's position implied that, if only Peking would change its "present course," the United States would become amenable to an improvement in relations. It was implicit in all his statements that he believed Peking was here to stay—which meant that he considered it the real government of China. This was a reversal of his May 1951 statement, when, as assistant secretary of state for Far Eastern affairs, he said that Peking "is not the government of China. It does not pass the first test. It is not Chinese." Assuming that Rusk and the Johnson administration as a whole considered Peking to be the real government of China, the fact that they continued formally to recognize the GRC as the sole legitimate government of China was due to considerations other than who actually governed China.

These considerations probably were: (1) The long-standing friendship for, and commitment to, the GRC. To have denied that this government was the government of all China would have been interpreted by it as an act of extreme hostility. (2) The continuing U.S. domestic political climate of hostility toward Peking.

Congress and public opinion remained resolutely opposed to any accommodation with Peking, at least until the tremendous costs of the Vietnam War finally prodded a substantial portion of Congress and the public, as well as the administration, to begin to reassess U.S. policy in Asia.

Rusk's demand that Peking renounce the use of force to take Taiwan met with no favorable response. Peking has consistently claimed the right to use force, if necessary, to "liberate" Taiwan. To her Taiwan is a part of China and the right to regain her own "stolen" territory is so fundamental that if necessary the use of force is justified. To suggest that the right to use force is lessened is to suggest that her claim to sovereignty over Taiwan is lessened.[132] For this reason, Washington's offer to improve relations provided Peking renounce the right to use force to take Taiwan appeared to Peking as a scheme designed to create "Two Chinas," of which one would be a U.S. client state on Taiwan. In commenting on the specific points Rusk made in his remarks to the House subcommittee in March 1966, the authoritative "Observer" wrote in the April 1, 1966, *Peking Review:*

> As a matter of fact, Rusk himself added an enlightening footnote to his" flexible policy." He said: One: the United States is "not prepared to surrender" Taiwan. Two: the United States will not change its attitude toward the restoration to China of its legitimate seat in the United Nations. This means that the United States will go on occupying China's territory and that it will cling to its position of hostility toward China. . . . This lets the cat out of the bag and shows what the U.S. "flexible policy" really means.[133]

Conclusion: The assumptions underlying the Johnson administration's policy toward China and Taiwan were essentially the same as those of the Kennedy administration. Johnson appeared to operate on the assumption that Peking was here to stay, but held that the United States should give full support to the GRC—even a GRC claiming to be the government of all China. That the Johnson administration at least formally recognized the GRC for what it claimed to be was specifically affirmed by Secretary of State Rusk in July 1966. During a visit to Taipei Rusk was asked by a GRC newsman: " . . . does the U.S. still consider the Nationalist government of China to be the sole and legitimate government of all China?" Rusk answered: "We recognize the Republic of China as the government of China with all of the implications that go with that."[134]

Whatever Rusk may really have believed in the 1960s concerning the rightful claimant to be the government of China, Peking received little encouragement to take this formal commitment to the GRC at anything other than its face value.

The logical contradiction inherent in supporting the GRC as the government of China while hoping that Peking would become more friendly was not resolved by the Johnson administration. The administration probably believed, or at least hoped, that, provided the United States stood firm, Peking would come to realize that her "aggressive" aims against Taiwan could not be achieved and that she would eventually come to accept some sort of "Two Chinas" arrangement in order to be re-admitted to the family of nations.

Nixon
Administration

UNLIKE HIS PREDECESSORS, President Nixon said a good deal about China and Taiwan before coming to office. As senator, vice-president, and private citizen he made his views known on a number of occasions. His pre-election comments could be described as "hard-line" in that they were strongly in favor of the policy of non-accommodation with Peking and full support for the Nationalist regime.

The extent to which the early Nixon differed with at least one of his predecessors—Kennedy—was revealed in their television campaign debate about Quemoy and Matsu. The question of the offshore islands, in fact, constituted perhaps the closest thing during the debates to a real issue of foreign policy. However, it should be pointed out that regarding the U.S. commitment to the GRC on Taiwan itself, or the aspirations of the native Taiwanese as opposed to those of the Mainlanders (aspirations which, of course, were not referred to at all), the two candidates did not differ.

During the second debate Kennedy said he thought it "unwise to take the chance of being dragged into a war which may lead to a world war over two islands which are not strategically defensible, which are not . . . essential to the defense of Formosa." [135] Nixon responded:

> . . . the question is not these two little pieces of real estate—they are unimportant. It isn't the few people who live on them—they are not too important. It's the principle involved.

These two islands are in the area of freedom. . . . We should not force our Nationalist allies to get off them and give them to the Communists.

If we do that we start a chain reaction because the Communists aren't after Quemoy and Matsu. They're after Formosa. [Kennedy's view] is the same kind of woolly thinking that led to disaster for America in Korea.[136]

In the third debate, Nixon further elaborated his views. He said that the surrender of the offshore islands, far from leading to peace, would in fact be

something that would lead, in my opinion, to war. . . . Now what do the Chinese Communists want? They don't want just Quemoy and Matsu. They don't want just Formosa. They want the world. And the question is if you surrender or indicate in advance that you are not going to defend any part of the free world, and you figure that is going to satisfy them, it doesn't satisfy them. It only whets their appetite. And then the question comes—when do you stop them?[137]

Thus the essence of Nixon's case at that time was that Quemoy and Matsu were part of the "Free World" and to surrender them would be appeasement which would whet the appetite of the aggressor as surely as Munich had spurred the ambitions of Hitler. Whether or not Peking might have a valid claim to the islands was not mentioned and in all likelihood was not even considered. The whole problem was seen in terms of halting Communist expansion beyond areas already under Communist control.

Before his election as president, Nixon was often accused by his opponents of partisanship in regard to foreign policy. There may have been some truth to the charge, at least in regard to China and the Far East. For instance, in October 1958 when the Democratic Advisory Council urged presentation of the Taiwan problem to the United Nations, Nixon called the statement an example of the "same defensive, defeatist, fuzzy-headed thinking which contributed to the loss of China and led to the Korean War."[138]

Nixon was not, of course, the only Republican leader to blame the Democrats for the "loss" of China. To attempt to hold him responsible in the 1970s for what he said in the climate of the 1950s is clearly unfair. However, a public official cannot completely escape his past statements, and any complete reversal of a publicly advocated position generally requires that he cover his tracks by some sort of rationalization for his changed position. At the very least, a firm public commitment to a certain course makes it more difficult to adopt a contrary one than would be the case if one's record on the question were blank. It is hard to believe that Nixon's twenty-some years of public and well-publicized commitment to a firm stand against Communist China and in favor of the GRC have had no effect on his thinking and actions since January 1969.

Despite Nixon's previous position, he has continued and even expanded the Kennedy and Johnson efforts to increase contact with Peking, provided this means no lessening of the U.S. commitment to the GRC. The administration has attributed lack of success of this approach to Peking's intransigence. As Secretary of State Rogers remarked in a speech in Australia in August 1969, Peking's "central position is that they will discuss nothing with us unless we first abandon support of our ally, the Republic of China. This we do not propose to do."[139]

Concerning the status of Communist China and Nationalist China in the United Nations, Nixon's initial position as president was presented in a news conference on January 27, 1969:

> The policy of this country and this administration at this time will be to continue to oppose Communist China's admission to the United Nations.
>
> There are several reasons for that:
>
> First, Communist China has not indicated any interest in becoming a member of the United Nations.
>
> Second, it has not indicated any intent to abide by the principles of the U.N. Charter and to meet the principles that new members admitted to the United Nations are supposed to meet.
>
> Finally, Communist China continues to call for expelling the Republic of China from the United Nations, and

the Republic of China has, as I think most know, been a member of the international community and has met its responsibilities without question over these past few years.[140]

Nixon has not publicly refuted this position since that time. However, if these three points accurately represented the thinking of Nixon and his administration in January 1969, by the time of the U.N. debate on the Chinese representation question in November 1970, substantial changes had taken place in administration thinking. By late 1970 it was obvious that Peking was once again (after several years of ambivalence during the Cultural Revolution) interested in being admitted to the United Nations—provided the GRC were expelled. The Nixon administration was well aware of Peking's renewed interest.

Nixon's second point in January 1969 had been, in essence, that Peking was not qualified for U.N. membership because of her aggressive nature. This was still a major part of the administration's case against Peking during the Fall 1969 U.N. China representation debates. At that time American representative J. Irving Whalley opposed Peking's entry in part because of her "policy of open hostility" toward her neighbors, her opposition to a peaceful settlement in Vietnam, the fact that she had "condemned efforts to end" the nuclear arms race, and her "unreasonable conditions" for joining the United Nations.[141] In other words, Whalley was saying, Peking was not fit for membership.

In 1970, however, American opposition was based solely on unwillingness to see the GRC expelled from the United Nations as the price for Peking's admittance. In an important speech on November 12, 1970, Christopher H. Phillips, the deputy permanent representative of the United States at the United Nations, avoided any repetition of the previous year's argument that the hostile nature of the Peking regime disqualified it for membership. Phillips remarked, "The fact of the matter is, the United States is as interested as any in this room to see the People's Republic of China play a constructive role among the family of nations." He agreed with those who said that Communist China was a "reality that cannot be ignored," and, in a passage of very real significance for Sino-American relations, said that it had become the policy of the United States to "move from an era of confrontation to an era of negotiation" with Communist China. Nevertheless, Phillips said, the interests of the United Nations would not be served by expelling the GRC, a U.N. member of good standing.[142] Thus, by November 1970, only the third of Nixon's January 1969 three points remained in effect.

Although the United States still opposed Peking's entry, the U.S. view of Peking's place in the world had changed significantly since the 1950s. Were it not for the Taiwan issue, Phillips was implying, the United States would not object to Peking's admission to the United Nations and would in all probability seek to normalize U.S.-Chinese relations.

The Nixon administration has gone farther than any previous administration in seeking to increase contacts with Peking without implying a lessening of commitment to the GRC. Secretary of State Rogers said in August 1969, "Communist China has long been too isolated. This is one of the reasons we have been seeking to open up channels of communication."[143] Reflecting this desire for increased communication, the administration in the summer of 1969 eased slightly the travel and trade restrictions in effect since 1950. Tourists could now bring $100 worth of Chinese Communist goods into the United States, and scholars, journalists, and scientists could validate their passports for travel to China. In December 1969 a further relaxation of trade restrictions permitted U.S. firms abroad to sell non-strategic goods to China and removed the $100 limit on Chinese goods brought into the United States.

By the end of 1970 it should have been clear to all concerned that the U.S. Government had come to accept the fact that Peking is here to stay. Richard Nixon, who for years had defended the GRC's right to speak for China, now based his policy on the assumption of Peking's permanence. Nixon's acceptance of the fact of Peking's rule of China by no means solved the United States' dilemma over what to do about Taiwan. The administration remained unwilling to renounce its commitment to the existing government on Taiwan and that government had no choice but to continue to claim to be the government of all China.

The import of the U.S. stand at the time of the U.N. debates in November 1970 was the heralding of a coming "Two Chinas" policy. This means in reality "one China and one Taiwan," but the concept probably allows the present government on Taiwan to continue for its own internal purposes to claim for a time to be that of all China. That some such change was coming was clear to Americans, to Peking, and to Taipei. There are indications that the United States has tried to persuade the GRC to soften its position to the extent of agreeing to remain in the United Nations even if the Communists are admitted,[144] but quite understandably these overtures have met with no known success. To agree to this would force the GRC to renounce the central claim that has sustained it ever since 1949—that the Peking authorities are temporary illegal usurpers and that only Taipei can legitimately represent China.

Acceptance of Nixon's apparent "Two Chinas" U.N. policy would probably be seen by the GRC as the first step toward its ultimate demise. It is argued later in this book that the GRC is, in immediate and realistic terms, concerned first of all with its own power position on Taiwan and that the regime's international position is of secondary importance, serving primarily as a prop to its internal position. If this is so, it would be more consistent for the GRC to choose to pull out of the United Nations than to agree to sit in a United Nations to which Peking had been admitted. It would probably be reasoned that an isolated GRC able to thumb its nose at the rest of the world would be better able to claim the moral right to continue to suppress the threat of Taiwanese self-determination than would a GRC which had compromised its sacred honor by admitting that Peking was a legitimate entity.

Ostensible moral justification for one's actions is vital in Chinese politics. The GRC claims to be the government of China, not Taiwan; the "temporary" suspension of elections on Taiwan and the suppression of Taiwanese political aspirations have been justified solely by this claim. To imply that Peking had a right to govern the other 99.7 percent of China—as would be the case with two "Chinese governments" in the United Nations —would be a major step toward negating the moral justification for continuing to suppress Taiwanese aspirations in the name of the greater cause of China. It is vital to the GRC, therefore, that U.S. overtures about a compromise on the Chinese representation question at the United Nations be rejected.

Of all the presidents since 1950, Nixon came into office with the strongest reputation as an opponent of Peking and a friend of Taipei. Yet he appears to have gone farther than any of his predecessors in seeking to establish channels of communication with Peking and in opening a wedge of doubt about U.S. support for the status claimed by the GRC. President Nixon's assessment of the U.S. interest in China is clearly different from that of Vice-President Nixon, ten years earlier. President Nixon himself has made no attempt to publicly explain away his earlier attitudes. Nor should he be expected to. A full explanation would require a thorough-going analysis of the climate of American opinion in the 1950s as contrasted with that of the early 1970s.

The early Nixon was an unabashed "Cold Warrior"; his motives were presumably a combination of conviction and politics. The Nixon of today is president of a country in which a large portion of the people are fed up with the Vietnam War; a country which desperately desires to reduce its commitments and risks in Asia, which no longer has an effective China lobby, and which has come to realize that there can be no real solution to the political problems of Asia as long as mainland China remains in embittered isolation.

The convictions of the American leaders and people today are significantly different from those that prevailed through the early 1960s. Because of this, the possibilities for movement on the China question are greatly increased. Congressional reaction to even the slightest hints of change during President Kennedy's term can be compared with the almost total lack of an adverse congressional reaction when in the fall of 1970 the Nixon administration clearly indicated its willingness to see Peking eventually sit alongside Taipei in the United Nations. Kennedy could not budge an inch on China; Nixon—if there were no Taiwan question—could guide the nation along a path leading at an early date to the normalization of relations with Peking.

Conclusion: It is clear that President Nixon now accepts the overwhelming likelihood of the permanence of the Peking government. It is also clear that the administration would like to improve relations with Peking, if for no other reason than that it is politically desirable to reduce U.S. risks and costs in Asia. Nevertheless, in regard to the U.S. commitment to the present government of Taiwan, Nixon has not yet shown any public sign of wavering from the policy handed down from the 1950s.

Summary and Analysis of the Assumptions Underlying U.S. Policy Toward Taiwan

THE ORIGINAL COMMITMENT to protect the GRC on Taiwan came as a result of the Korean War. As of June 27, 1950, Truman and Acheson most certainly did not consider the Chiang Kai-shek government to be either democratic (i.e., "Free China" in any meaningful sense) or qualified to represent the people of mainland China. However, a direct result of the decision to "neutralize the Taiwan Strait" was to give Chiang the opportunity to solidify both his hold over the island and the claim that his government was the sole legitimate government of China. The June 27 action was almost certainly conceived as a temporary measure to stabilize the existing situation in the Taiwan Strait for the duration of the Korean War, rather than a long-range plan to perpetuate on Taiwan a rival "Free Chinese" government that would speak for China in the councils of the world for decades to come.

It was during the Eisenhower years that the largely fortuitous ramifications of the neutralization of the Taiwan Strait came to be thought of as immutable elements of U.S. China policy. Although Eisenhower and Dulles did at times show doubts about the stated belief that the Communist regime was a "passing phase" and that it would eventually be replaced by the "Free Chinese" on Taiwan, the China policy that developed from 1951 to 1960 was explicitly founded upon the idea of support for the GRC as an entity whose fundamental role was to challenge the legitimacy of the government in Peking. U.S. spokesmen said repeatedly that it was the policy of the United States to work for the elimination of communism in China and to support the GRC as a "free" alternative government for China.

In contrast to Secretary Dulles and the State Department under Dulles' influence, Eisenhower himself stressed the importance of Taiwan as a segment of the strategic island defense chain rather than the hope for GRC recovery of the mainland. But such a strategic interest would not of itself appear to demand support for a regime on Taiwan claiming legitimacy over all China. It is conceivable that Eisenhower saw the mainland recovery theme essentially as a morale-boosting device not necessarily related to the real prospects of the GRC for replacing the Peking regime—that although he knew the mainland recovery theme was a "myth" he believed Taiwan's strategic value was so great that it overrode the importance of publicly replacing this myth with a statement of reality.

When Eisenhower argued that the mainland recovery theme was essential to maintaining the morale of the "garrison and population" on Taiwan, he implied that this included not just the Mainlander refugee troops, but also the native Taiwanese population. It is argued here that the native Taiwanese would like to abandon the mainland recovery dream, and that, if given the chance, they would readily divest themselves of the mainland recovery "stepping stones" (the offshore islands).

If this is so, Eisenhower's reasoning was based on inaccurate assumptions for he argued that although holding the offshore islands greatly increased the risk of an American war with China, it was necessary to hold them as essential to maintaining morale on Taiwan. If the morale of Chiang's army were destroyed, he contended, there would be no incentive for the population on Taiwan to resist a Communist Chinese takeover and Taiwan would be lost as a link in the "Free World's" island defense chain.

Eisenhower's reasoning is incompatible with the interpretation that the native Taiwanese are united in opposing a Communist Chinese takeover, that they desire political independence from China, and that they believe that keeping alive the futile mainland recovery dream (with its stated goal of an eventual showdown with Peking) is in fact the single factor most likely to bring about Peking's ultimate control over the island.

Even if Eisenhower had been convinced that the Taiwanese would have chosen independence if given a free choice, he might still have chosen to support the GRC for strategic reasons. He might have reasoned that the strategic advantages of having a solidly entrenched and anti-Communist "Free Chinese" ally were so great that there was no choice but to ignore the just desires of the Taiwanese for the immediate future.

If reality had been squarely faced, and if at the same time an attempt had been made to instill a little meaningful democracy into the Taiwanese scene, a process would have been set in motion which could have ended with the realization of a popular government determined to remain out of Peking's hands and friendly to the "Free World". Such a process might also have ended, however, in Mainlander-Taiwanese bloodshed and a chaotic situation that could have been exploited by the Chinese Communists.

However, the weight of the evidence is clearly against the view that the Eisenhower administration carefully examined the Taiwanese side and then with cool calculation chose to back the GRC instead. Rather, available information including the writings of the president himself indicates that the administration hardly looked at the Taiwanese case. There is, in fact, little indication of awareness that a Taiwanese case existed.

It seems clear that the decision-making level of the Eisenhower administration was in fact not very concerned about the internal political realities of Taiwan, particularly in regard to the overriding political fact on Taiwan—the Mainlander-Taiwanese split. This lack of concern was the product of several factors. Perhaps the most important was the climate of American opinion at that time, with its strongly anti-Peking feeling; the pro-Nationalist sentiment was a readily explainable reaction to this. Pressures from Congress pushed the administration to take a hard line toward Peking and to continue full support of the Nationalists.

As discussed above, on-the-spot State Department reporting, at least that of Ambassador Karl Rankin, was openly biased in favor of the official "Free Chinese" position and revealed a rather startling lack of curiosity about the 85 percent Taiwanese majority. It is easy to understand, given the political and bureaucratic pressures under which the administration operated, that any tendency to develop a line of inquiry possibly leading to a fundamental re-examination of the assumptions behind the policy that evolved after June 1950 would have been consciously or subconsciously nipped in the bud.

In the 1950s, it can be concluded, U.S. policy was founded essentially on two major assumptions: (1) the GRC had a real chance of eventually replacing the Communist regime, or at least of eventually having an influence on mainland developments of benefit to U.S. interests; and (2) if Taiwan were to continue to have a stable anti-Communist government, there was no alternative to full U.S. backing for the existing Nationalist government.

U.S. policy toward China and Taiwan underwent no fundamental change during the 1960s. Communist China remained unrecognized and the United States continued to expend great effort and political capital to keep China out of the United Nations. The United States still recognizes the GRC not only as the government of Taiwan but, at least formally, as the legitimate government of China. Today, the interests of the native Taiwanese may get increasing attention in private discussion among American officials, but as long as the GRC is recognized as the government of Taiwan, the fundamental Taiwanese political aim of self-determination must of necessity receive no formal recognition in U.S. policy.

It can be stated with reasonable confidence that since the early 1960s the U.S. Government has no longer assumed that communism in China is a "passing phase," nor that the GRC's chances of regaining the mainland are sufficiently great for the United States to rely on this hope as the cornerstone of its long-term China policy. If it is assumed now that Peking is for all intents and purposes permanent, there must be some other rationale for a policy of support for a government of Taiwan that claims to be the sole legitimate government of all China.[145]

What new assumptions could justify a continuation of the policy handed down from the 1950s? Here it is necessary to speculate since no one has promulgated a new set of official rationales. The postulated new assumptions can be divided into two categories: (1) those concerning the U.S. interest (i.e., U.S. policy goals), and (2) those concerning the political realities of Communist China and Taiwan. (It should be kept in mind that U.S. thinking about China and Taiwan is presently, in late 1970, in a state of flux. The attempt here is to assess U.S. thinking as it existed at the end of the 1960s and the beginning of the 1970s.)

(1) U.S. Goals.

(a) To avoid all-out, unlimited war with China. To date this has been achieved in regard to Taiwan primarily through deterrence of a Chinese attack rather than through any serious attempt to settle the fundamental political issues.

(b) To keep Taiwan out of Communist hands, for an amalgam of strategic, ideological, and moral reasons. The United States has gone to great expense to keep Taiwan out of Communist hands for the last twenty years and would not lightly abandon the island, even if the United States were convinced that the main cause of conflict between the United States and China could be removed by abandoning Taiwan to the Communists.

(c) To keep alive a "Free Chinese" alternative to communism. Although it is clear that present top-level U.S. policy makers do not hold out any real chance of the GRC recovering the mainland, they may still believe that the mere existence of a noncommunist Chinese society and government could eventually have a beneficial effect on Chinese developments. They may reason that if the people on the mainland are aware that there exists a Chinese society which is more prosperous, more open, and less politically demanding on the citizen's day-to-day life, the mainland people might eventually put pressure on their own government to move in the same direction. They may also feel that keeping alive a "Free Chinese" alternative is of some value in keeping the Overseas Chinese in Southeast Asia from becoming too pro-Peking.[146]

(d) To maintain the commitment to Chiang Kai-shek and his government. Whatever policy makers today might think of Chiang Kai-shek, the United States has been profoundly committed to his regime—a commitment dating from the time the United States entered World War II. There is no doubt that even today a good portion of the Congress and the public would be very disturbed if the United States suddenly abandoned Chiang.

(e) Some U.S. policy makers may feel that the Taiwanese desire for self-determination is just and reasonable and may hope that it can eventually be realized. However, they probably see its realization as gradual, and over a long period, if at all. Time, they may believe, will ultimately bring the Taiwanese majority into a position of dominance, thereby removing the undemocratic basis of present GRC rule. It is probably felt that the United States can or should do little to further Taiwanese control. There is no emotional commitment to the Taiwanese, such as there has been to Chiang Kai-shek and his government; at least some U.S. officials may have been conditioned to think of the Taiwanese as potential pawns in any future settlement with Peking rather than as a political community which must enjoy the right to determine its own future.

The question of what the United States should do with, for, or to the native Taiwanese population appears to hold very low priority when compared to questions of U.S. relations with Communist China, U.S. relations with the Chinese Nationalists, and overall U.S. aims in Asia. It also seems that in contrast with the major commitments made to the governments of South Korea, Thailand, South Vietnam, or Nationalist China the United States is far from eager to undertake any new commitment to protect a hypothetical, future Taiwanese-controlled Taiwan.

(2) Assumptions concerning the political realities of Communist China and Taiwan.

(a) The great majority of the Chinese people currently accept the legitimacy of the Peking regime, but there is a good chance that they wouldn't if they saw an alternative. It is likely that people high in the U.S. Government still feel that there is something unnatural about communism in China and that if given a free choice the Chinese people would voluntarily choose something closer to the kind of "Free Chinese" society that exists on Taiwan.[147]

(b) At least some people in the U.S. Government probably feel that although it is impossible to determine precisely the intensity of Chinese Communist feelings concerning Taiwan, it is unlikely that Taiwan is, as the Chinese have often said, their fundamental issue with the United States. Surely if Taiwan—a relatively insignificant, small, and over-populated island—were the main issue, China's attitude could not have been as hostile as it has been for over twenty years. Compared with the goals of world communism and Asian domination, the Taiwan issue cannot seem all that important to Peking. Therefore, these officials may argue that although the Taiwan problem is certainly very important there is no pressing need to solve it prior to some indication of a broader willingness on the part of Peking to reduce tensions with the United States.

(c) The Taiwanese people would probably like to control their own affairs, but given the lack of an organized Taiwanese independence movement on Taiwan it can be assumed that this desire is not very strong. U.S. policy makers probably reason that any people who strongly dislike their present government and desire to replace it with one more responsive to their own wishes would not be as docile as the Taiwanese have been.

(d) Although the United States treats Chiang Kai-shek as a long-standing, loyal ally, it cannot really trust him or his regime. U.S. China/Taiwan specialists may fear that if the United States attempts to force Chiang to change the nature of his rule, he might act rashly. Some at least may feel that whereas Chiang is the "faithful ally" of the United States as long as the United States plays his game, if the United States attempted to back genuine representative government for Taiwan or publicly refuted Chiang's mainland claims, Chiang might be driven to use his ultimate sanction of blackmail—to make a deal with Peking without reference to the wishes of the U.S. Government or the population of Taiwan.

If these assumptions represent current U.S. thinking, U.S. policy makers could conclude the following: (1) The policy handed down from the 1950s was originally based in part on a myth. (2) Despite this fact, the uncertainties involved in any attempt to force the GRC to openly abandon its mainland recovery myth or to allow the development of a genuinely representative government on Taiwan would not justify risking the loss of Taiwan's present stability (whether or not imposed by force). (3) Communist China has given no clear indication that a transfer of power from the GRC to a Taiwanese government would create conditions for fundamentally improving Sino-American relations. (4) China demands control over Taiwan, but the United States is unwilling to grant this. There is, therefore, no urgent need to change present U.S. policy regarding support of the GRC as opposed to the interests of the Taiwanese because this would not remove the basic unacceptable Chinese Communist demand. (5) The United States would be foolish to undertake major political risks on behalf of a Taiwanese population which appears to have docilely submitted to GRC rule.

The argument is often heard that the United States need not insist that its allies be democratic and that the U.S. strategic interest may override concern for the level of freedom and democracy in an allied state—particularly if that state is a small one which is threatened by Communist aggression. Specifically, in regard to Taiwan, it is argued that although the United States might like to see a more democratic government there, considerations of security must come first. However, the preceding pages suggest that the U.S. commitment to the GRC became fixed in the 1950s in large part because that regime was considered genuinely "free," if not quite an electoral democracy of the American type. The U.S. policy makers of the 1950s indicated over and over their admiration and respect for the "Free Chinese" government and society, and their statements seem to have been quite sincere. Even today the GRC continues to receive much praise from U.S. leaders, although more is now said about economic than political achievements.

Observers of U.S. policy toward the GRC should be aware of the contradiction in two of the arguments that have most often been used in support of that policy: first, that the United States should support the GRC because it is free and democratic; and, second, that the U.S. strategic interest demands support for the GRC despite the fact that the GRC is not free and democratic.

U.S. Assumptions About Communist China Which Relate to Policy Toward Taiwan

U.S. policy toward Taiwan there are two main questions that involve Communist China. One is the degree to which the Communist government is stable, entrenched, and accepted by the Chinese people. This relates directly to the prospects for the GRC to make good on its claim to be the legitimate government of China. The second question is the extent to which Taiwan is important to the Chinese Communists and the significance of Taiwan in relations between Communist China and the United States.

The stability of the Peking regime and its susceptibility to being overthrown by the Chinese Nationalists will not be examined in detail here. Numerous volumes have been written on the stability and degree of acceptance of the Communist government and suffice it to say that it is the overwhelming conclusion of informed observers that at least for the foreseeable future it is here to stay. Almost all works by serious students about mainland China today carry the implicit assumption that their authors are dealing with a subject with a future rather than a transitory phenomenon.

For the purposes of this discussion it is assumed that barring totally unforeseen events the Communist regime is well entrenched; furthermore, even in the unlikely event that it collapses from within, its replacement would probably grow out of groups existing on the mainland rather than the Nationalist regime of Chiang Kai-shek. Although this point may appear in 1970 to be a statement of the obvious, the contrary proposition—that the GRC had a good chance of returning to the mainland—was a guiding assumption behind the policy that was formulated in the 1950s and which is still followed today.

In contrast to the question of the stability of the Communist regime, Peking's interest in Taiwan is a matter of considerable debate among both governmental and academic observers of China. Some contend that Taiwan cannot be as important to the Chinese Communists as Peking says. They argue instead that the Chinese, for whatever reasons they may have, do not want to improve relations with the United States at this time and that because of this they use the Taiwan issue largely as a pretext.[148] Peking's demand that all other issues with the United States must wait until the Taiwan question is settled is dismissed by these observers as a pretext for maintaining a high level of hostility and tension until other, more important, Communist aims are achieved.

It is argued by those who take this position that to treat Taiwan as the overriding issue to which a solution should be sought as early as possible in order to begin working toward an eventual modus vivendi with China would be playing into Chinese hands. In such circumstances the United States would be forced to make concessions on Taiwan without winning any agreement from the Chinese to moderate their world-wide aggressive aims.

Those who argue this viewpoint can find supporting evidence in certain Chinese statements about the United Nations in the last half of the 1960s. Such statements demanded that the United Nations, in effect, alter its structure and nature before the Chinese would deign to enter. Undoubtedly Peking's hostile and contemptuous attitude toward the United Nations during this period was on President Nixon's mind when he contended in January 1969 that Peking had "not indicated any interest in becoming a member of the United Nations." A typical statement from a *People's Daily* editorial in 1965, was:

To return to the path of its purposes and principles, the United Nations must break the U.S. control, correct all its mistakes and undergo a thorough reorganization and reform. Expelling the members of the Chiang Kai-shek clique from the United Nations and restoring to China its legitimate rights is an indispensable step for the United Nations to correct its mistakes and undergo a thorough reorganization. But it is far from enough to do this only. The United Nations must also resolutely condemn U.S. imperialism, the biggest aggressor of our time, and cancel its slanderous resolution condemning China and the Democratic People's Republic of Korea as aggressors, and all its other erroneous resolutions.[149]

This could be interpreted to mean that to the Chinese a resolution of the Taiwan issue in the United Nations is only a first step in a broader policy aimed at U.S. "imperialism." If these are their priorities in regard to the United Nations, one might argue, the Chinese may hold the same priorities in regard to the Cold War confrontation in general.

It can be pointed out, however, that prior to the Cultural Revolution Peking stressed the single issue that the United Nations must expel the "Chiang Kai-shek gang." With this proviso, Peking made it quite clear that she was not only willing but eager to enter the United Nations. Why did her attitude change in the mid-1960s? Was the earlier obsession with the Chiang "gang" a pretext for avoiding the moral sanctions she might face as a U.N. member? Have the more recent broadsides exposed the true nature of Peking's hostility toward the United Nations? Or is it that after some fifteen years of beating her head against the walls of the United Nations, her frustration reached the point where she reacted by saying, in effect, "To hell with the United Nations?"

Compare the above quoted 1965 *People's Daily* editorial with the remarks of Foreign Minister Ch'en Yi in 1961, before the Cultural Revolution hardened Peking's position on the United Nations. Ch'en said:

Some people assert that the People's Republic of China is

not willing to enter the United Nations, this is entirely groundless. The United Nations, under domination of the United States, has persisted in regarding a handful of U.S.-kept Chiang Kai-shek elements as China's representatives and letting them usurp China's seat. This is the basic reason why the rightful position of the People's Republic of China in the United Nations has not yet been restored. Now, some people try to refuse to restore to the People's Republic of China her rightful position in the United Nations by retaining the Chiang Kai-shek elements there, while asserting that the People's Republic of China is not willing to enter the United Nations. This is a plot.[150]

Peking in 1970 returned to the more moderate attitude indicated in Ch'en's 1961 statement. It has once again become apparent that Peking wants to claim the U.N. seat she feels she rightly deserves.

An alternative view of basic Chinese aims is that Taiwan is so fundamental an issue with the Chinese that, as long as the United States continues to support a rival Chinese regime on Taiwan there is nothing that the United States could do elsewhere to bring about a fundamental improvement in relations with China. For instance, even if the United States withdrew completely from Korea, Vietnam, and elsewhere on the Asian mainland, basic Chinese attitudes toward the United States would not be altered if the United States continued to back the GRC on Taiwan.

The two top-level Chinese spokesmen who have probably had the most frequent and most intimate contact with non-Communist foreign visitors, and whose statements have generally been regarded as relatively candid, are Premier Chou En-lai and Foreign Minister Ch'en Yi. Both have reportedly gone out of their way in private discussions to stress the fundamental importance of the Taiwan issue to Peking.

Edgar Snow has had more face-to-face contact with Communist leaders than has any other American. Snow's conclusion is that Taiwan is the fundamental issue to be resolved before there can be any normalization of relations between China and the United States. During visits to China in 1960 and 1965 Snow talked with several leaders, including Mao Tse-tung, Ch'en Yi, and Chou En-lai. His conversations were particularly detailed in the case of Chou, who told him:

> It is inconceivable that a peace pact can be concluded without diplomatic relations between China and the United States.
>
> It is also inconceivable that there can be diplomatic relations between China and the United States without a settlement of the dispute between the two countries in the Taiwan region.[151]

Mao, Ch'en, and Chou, according to Snow, all insisted to him that to compromise with the United States on Taiwan was impossible as long as U.S. "armed intervention" continued there.[152]

Kenneth Young, in his thorough review of the Sino-American ambassadorial talks in Geneva and Warsaw,[153] makes it clear that the fundamental obstacle to progress in the talks has been Chinese intransigence on the Taiwan issue. Young concludes that the Chinese entered and conducted the talks "primarily—even exclusively" to gain U.S. concessions on Taiwan.[154] Young points out that Peking has demanded U.S. agreement in principle to withdraw from Taiwan as an absolute pre-condition for discussion and agreement on any other issue.[155] In May 1966 Chou En-lai tied the ambassadorial talks to the Taiwan question. He said that China had been

> demanding through negotiations, that the United States withdraw all its armed forces from Taiwan province and the Taiwan Straits, and she has held talks with the United States for more than ten years . . . on this question of principle, which admits of no concession whatsoever.[156]

Secretary of State Rusk confirmed the importance of Taiwan in the talks in his March 16, 1966, statement of policy:

> . . . the talks have, so far, given no evidence of a shift or easing in Peiping's hostility toward the United States and its bellicose doctrines of world revolution. Indeed, the Chinese

Communists have consistently demanded, privately as well as publicly, that we let them have Taiwan. And when we say that we will not abandon the 12 or 13 million people on Taiwan against their will, they say that, until we change our minds about that, no improvement in relations is possible.

Today we and Peiping are as far apart on matters of fundamental policy as we were seventeen years ago.[157]

The United States is not the only nation whose experience in negotiations with Peking has exposed it to the full brunt of Chinese intransigence over Taiwan. Canadian sources have said that during the twenty months of negotiations in Stockholm that preceded the establishment of relations between China and Canada in October 1970 the Taiwan issue so dominated the meetings that the participants never got around to the mundane arrangements necessary for establishing diplomatic missions in their respective capitals.[158] Canada refused to grant that Taiwan belonged to Peking and finally agreed that while recognizing Peking as the sole government of China, Canada would "take note" that Peking claimed sovereignty over Taiwan. The use of this formula will probably become widespread as more and more countries establish relations with Peking.

In 1960, Chou En-lai made the following remarks to British television correspondent Felix Greene:

So long as the United States continues to occupy Taiwan, there can be no basic improvement in the relations between China and the United States. . . The U.S. Government is occupying China's territory Taiwan with its armed forces and blocking the Chinese Government from exercising its sovereignty in Taiwan. There is only one way to settle this question. The U.S. Government must agree to withdraw all its armed forces from Taiwan and the Taiwan Straits. . . The United States seeks to set up what they call an "independent state" of Taiwan or a "Sino-Formosan nation," or to conduct what they call a "plebiscite," in Taiwan, or even to place Taiwan "under trusteeship," and so on. All this is aimed at dismembering Chinese territory, violating China's sovereign rights and legalizing the seizure of Taiwan by the United States.[159]

Foreign Minister Ch'en Yi has been as explicit as Chou En-lai about the fundamental importance of Taiwan. In April 1961, in response to a question concerning the future of Sino-American relations put to him by a *New York Times* correspondent during Ch'en's visit to Indonesia, Ch'en said:

> Sino-American relations are a matter of the United States adopting an imperialist policy towards China. Whether this will change or not, it is up to the United States. We persist in the position that the Seventh Fleet must be withdrawn from the Taiwan Straits. This ought not to be a difficult thing for the United States to do.[160]

In June 1961 Ch'en told a Canadian newsman:

> The United States has occupied China's territory Taiwan by force. And the Chinese people are resolutely opposed to this policy of the United States. Such is the essence of the Sino-American dispute. If the United States withdraws all its armed forces from Taiwan and the Taiwan Straits and stops interfering in China's internal affairs, it will be entirely possible to settle the dispute peacefully. We hope that the dispute will be settled peacefully and we have worked for this. Indeed, we have been doing so for eleven years. But whether there will be a settlement depends entirely on the United States. Taiwan was already an inalienable part of China's territory long before Columbus discovered the new continent of America. We are deeply convinced that no matter how long Taiwan may continue to be seized by the United States, it will in the end return to the motherland.[161]

Ch'en Yi told a group of Japanese journalists in 1964:

> The Chinese Government has on many occasions expressed its readiness to settle Sino-U.S. disputes through peaceful negotiations, including the question of the withdrawal of U.S. armed forces from Taiwan and the Straits of Taiwan and

not to resort to force. The Sino-American talks which have
continued for eight years deal mainly with this question. The
principle we have put forward at the Sino-American talks
is very simple, consisting of only two items: first, China and
the United States to coexist peacefully according to the
Five Principles; second, the U.S. Government to guarantee
to withdraw its armed forces from China's Taiwan Province
and the Straits of Taiwan. . . .[162]

In December 1966 Ch'en told a Brazilian interviewer:

In the last ten years we have had ambassadorial-level meetings with the United States which could have brought forth
a Chinese [-American] agreement. But invariably the representatives of Washington reject the precepts of peaceful
coexistence and refuse to withdraw their forces from Formosa and the Strait of Taiwan. . . . We must first resolve
the most important problem, Taiwan. . . [163]

Editorials in leading Chinese newspapers and periodicals
have also emphasized the importance of Taiwan in Sino-American relations. A May 1964 editorial in the *People's Daily*
("China's Sovereignty Over Taiwan Brooks No Intervention")
stated bluntly that the present unfriendly relationship between
China and the United States "is entirely the result of U.S. government policy of hostility to China and occupation of the Chinese
territory of Taiwan."[164]

In April 1966 the authoritative "Observer" said in the
Peking Review:

The source of all the [Sino-American] tension springs from
the extremely hostile policy that the US. Government per-
sistently pursues towards China, and primarily because the
United States is forcefully occupying China's province of
Taiwan. So long as the U.S. Government does not change
its hostile policy towards China and refuses to pull its armed
forces out of Taiwan and the Taiwan Straits, the normalization of Sino-American relations is entirely out of the question.[165]

If it is argued that Taiwan is the fundamental problem to be resolved before Peking will become interested in an improvement in relations with the United States, one still faces the question of just what it is about the Taiwan situation that is so utterly unbearable to Peking. Does Peking feel that she cannot live without actual physical control over Taiwan? Or is the real issue that of the existence on Taiwan of a regime, dependent on U.S. support, which claims the right to overthrow the Peking regime and which is still recognized (thanks to U.S. efforts) by a number of countries as the legitimate government of China representing all China in the United Nations and most other international organizations?

There can be little doubt that Peking has up to the present time felt that her demands both for the elimination of a rival Chinese regime and for actual occupation of Taiwan have been just. However, it is reasonable to speculate that the difference between the two demands (or two aspects of the one demand) is apparent to at least the more worldly Chinese Communist leaders. Whereas there can be no doubt in their minds about whether Peking or Taipei is qualified to claim legitimacy as the government of China, they cannot be unaware of the fact that Taiwan has been effectively cut off culturally, economically, and politically from mainland China ever since the Japanese occupation began in 1895. Unless the Communist leaders are totally isolated from reality they must be aware that the Taiwanese have more than just a typical Chinese provincial feeling of separate identity; they cannot be unaware that the Taiwanese justifiably feel a desire to have at least some say in the determination of their own future.

The possibility that the Taiwanese might desire some sort of separate status occurred to the Communist leadership as early as the 1930's. As quoted in *Red Star Over China*, Edgar Snow asked Mao Tse-tung what he thought China should do about the territories she had lost to Japan. Mao answered:

Manchuria must be regained. We do not, however, include Korea, formerly a Chinese colony, but when we have re-established the independence of the lost territories of China, and if the Koreans wish to break away from the chains of

Japanese imperialism, we will extend them our enthusiastic
help in their struggle for independence. The same thing ap-
plies for Formosa.[166]

Mao's apparent willingness to let Taiwan go was in contrast to his
expectations concerning Outer Mongolia: "When the people's
revolution has been victorious in China the Outer Mongolian republic will automatically become a part of the Chinese federation,
at their own will."[167] Mao may have changed his generous attitude
toward Taiwan since then, of course, but there is every reason to
believe that, despite the current official propaganda line, responsible Communist leaders are aware that the Taiwan situation in-
volves more than U.S. and Chinese Nationalist suppression of
a native Taiwanese desire to return to the Chinese motherland.

Since 1949 Peking leaders have not publicly discussed the
complexities of the Taiwan issue in terms of the intensity or just-
ness of the Taiwanese desire for separatism. Assuming they are
aware of this desire, there would remain good reasons for their not
dwelling on it. They do indeed hope to control Taiwan, and any
public recognition on their part of a desire for Taiwanese sep-
eration might well give a major boost to separatist tendencies.
The Chinese probably want to keep their options open for the
present, and this can best be done by maintaining their present
intransigence on the Taiwan issue.

For Peking at this time to provide any encouragement at
all for the trend toward Taiwanese separation might tend to permanently foreclose the option of ultimate Chinese sovereignty or
control over Taiwan. Continuing for the present her uncompromising demand for Taiwan, on the other hand, should mean that
there would remain for Peking at least the possibility of Taiwan's
reversion to China when what the Chinese Communists see as the
inevitable demise of the GRC finally occurs.

Even if under certain circumstances an independent or genuinely autonomous Taiwan would be something that Peking could
live with, an independent Taiwan closely allied with the United
States would not be. There would be good reasons for Peking to remain intransigent in her unwillingness to compromise on
Taiwan for the present. It would be logical for the Chinese to

stand pat until they receive firm guarantees for a withdrawal of
the U.S. military presence from Taiwan. To soften their demands
now might encourage the Taiwanese to attempt to secure their
independence with a continuing U.S. shield and might convince
the United States that it could with minimum risk extend indefi-
nitely its mutual defense arrangements with Taiwan.

If the Chinese are in fact willing to consider granting Taiwan
a meaningful degree of independence or autonomy, it is safe to
say that they want to do it voluntarily rather than to have such
a solution imposed by U.S. military might. If the final status of
Taiwan is either to be dictated by Peking or settled by a direct
agreement between Peking and the authorities (whether present
or future) on Taiwan—these are almost certainly the only two
prospects that Peking would be willing to consider—Peking must
keep a firm grip on the direction taken at present by the debate
over Taiwan's future status. Her current intransigent demands
assure that any proposed settlement that ignores Peking's interest
in Taiwan is unlikely to be considered by anyone as a permanent and unchallenged solution to the problem of the status of
Taiwan.

Since October 1970 it can no longer be said that Peking's
demands concerning Taiwan have been totally uncompromising.
In accepting that Canada need only "take note" of Peking's claim
to sovereignty over the island, Peking backed off from its original
negotiating demand that Canada agree that Taiwan belonged to
China. This "compromise" in no way reduced Peking's claim to
Taiwan, but was an implicit recognition of the strength of international support for keeping Taiwan separate from the mainland.
And it indicated that other aims (in this case the establishment of
diplomatic relations with Canada and other countries which might
hope to use the same formula) can under certain conditions take
precedence over the assertion of the moral claim to Taiwan.

Peking must have weighed carefully the prospect that this
compromise would be interpreted abroad as a softening of her
stand—a potentially dangerous move in a contest in which one
is relying on willpower and moral certitude as important weapons.
The longer Taiwan and mainland China remain apart the more
divergent their societies may become and the more a separate

Taiwan will be accepted internationally as part of the status quo. Peking's compromise with Canada implied a willingness to postpone for an indeterminate period the consummation of Peking's claim to sovereignty over Taiwan. In so doing Peking ran the risk, without doubt knowingly, of increasing those tendencies and pressures that are favorable to a continued separate status for Taiwan.

Assuming that Peking is willing to use the Canadian formula with additional countries, it may yet be unwilling to apply it to the United States and Japan. These are the only countries that have the power or influence, whether existing or potential, to intervene effectively to thwart Chinese designs on the island. For Peking to compromise her stand to secure recognition from Canada or Italy, neither of which can materially affect the ultimate outcome, is one thing. To retreat the same distance in direct confrontation with the two powers that have a commitment backed up by real (or potential) power to keep Taiwan out of Chinese hands would be more likely to give the appearance that China was already consciously moving in the direction of ultimately giving up the contest.

Looking again at the above-quoted statements of Chinese leaders concerning Taiwan, one will notice that the emphasis is not on the communization (or "liberation") of Taiwan. Rather, insofar as there is a specific demand, the emphasis is strongly on the withdrawal of U.S. forces. Chou En-lai in May 1966 said the aim of the ambassadorial talks had been to get the United States to "withdraw all its armed forces from Taiwan and the Taiwan Straits." In 1960 he told Felix Green that "So long as the United States continues to occupy Taiwan, there can be no basic improvement in the relations between China and the United States."

Edgar Snow concluded from his talks with Mao, Chou, and Ch'en Yi that China could not compromise with the United States on Taiwan as long as the "U.S. armed intervention" continued there. In April 1961 Ch'en Yi told the *New York Times* correspondent that China "persist[s] in the position that the Seventh Fleet must be withdrawn from the Taiwan Straits," adding that this "ought not to be a difficult thing for the United States to do."

In 1964 Ch'en told the Japanese journalists that there were only two conditions for peaceful settlement of disputes between the United States and China: first, agreement to "co-exist peacefully"; second, for the "U.S. Government to guarantee to withdraw its armed forces from China's Taiwan Province and the Straits of Taiwan." In December 1966 Ch'en told the Brazilian interviewer that the ambassadorial talks had failed to lead to an improvement in relations with the United States because the United States "refuse[d] to withdraw their forces from Taiwan and the Strait of Taiwan."

Although Chinese leaders have consistently demanded eventual withdrawal of U.S. armed forces from Taiwan, they have hinted that the withdrawal need not be immediate—that it could, in fact, be spread over a substantial period of time. For instance, as the since-purged P'eng Te-huai said in an appeal for the co-operation of KMT officials in 1958, "Of course we are not advising you to break with the Americans right away. That would be an unrealistic idea."[168]

According to Edgar Snow, Chou En-lai put it in the following terms in 1960: "The United States must agree to withdraw its armed forces from Taiwan and the Taiwan Straits. As to the specific steps on when and how to withdraw, they are matters for subsequent discussion"[169]

Ch'en Yi told the Japanese journalists that the United States need only "guarantee" to withdraw its forces, implying that the actual withdrawal need not be immediate. These hints indicate that at least the more realistic Chinese leaders are aware that the United States may not be able to simply abandon Taiwan immediately and unconditionally.

What flexibility would the United States have and what steps could be taken to protect the interests of the people of Taiwan once the United States "guaranteed" to withdraw its forces and began the "subsequent discussion" suggested by Chou to Edgar Snow? How long could the "specific steps on when and how to withdraw" be extended—for months, years, or decades? Has the United States seriously discussed these matters with the Chinese? There is no indication that it has.

In a speech in February 1967, U. Alexis Johnson, who personally represented the United States in the Sino-American ambassadorial talks from 1953 to 1958, summarized the U.S. experience in negotiations with the Chinese concerning Taiwan:

> . . . I proposed that while fully maintaining whatever principles they desired with respect to Taiwan, they would simply say that they would not use force in the situation, and I offered to make a reciprocal statement on behalf of the United States.
>
> Ambassador Wang resisted then and Peking still stoutly resists this proposition, taking the position in effect that if they decide to do so they are fully entitled to seize Taiwan by force. They insisted then and still insist that the people of Taiwan and the Government of the Republic of China on Taiwan have no rights except what Peking chooses to give them and that the only answer is for the United States to withdraw its recognition and treaty commitments with regard to Taiwan so that Peking can have a free hand to settle questions in any way it chooses.[170]

Johnson's comments indicate that the specific Chinese demand is for the sovereign right to determine Taiwan's status. Does this mean that Peking demands actual control over Taiwan or merely that she insists that there can be no final settlement of Taiwan's status that does not have her consent? Johnson's remarks do not indicate that the Chinese have revealed what "rights" Peking might ultimately "choose to give" Taiwan, nor that the United States has explored this question in depth with the Chinese.[171]

The explicit demand of responsible Chinese leaders has been, in effect, "the United States must agree to get out of Taiwan." It has not been, "the United States (or anybody) must give us unconditional control over Taiwan." While recognizing that the Chinese almost certainly do desire to see Taiwan incorporated as a regular province of the People's Republic of China, the remarks of Chou, Ch'en, and others are not incompatible with an interpretation that what the Chinese really think and want is as follows:

(1) The GRC must be eliminated as a rival claimant to legitimacy as the government of China, and Peking's right to speak for China in all forums must be recognized absolutely.

(2) Had it not been for U.S. intervention, China would have

occupied ("liberated") Taiwan in 1950 or soon thereafter. This "imperialist aggression" against China must be erased before any solution to the Taiwan problem is possible; that is, the United States must within a reasonably short time, to be decided by negotiations, withdraw its forces from Taiwan and the Taiwan Strait.

(3) Once the United States withdraws or agrees to withdraw, underlying political forces and interests can come into play. One of these is the historical Chinese claim to sovereignty over Taiwan. Another is the political aspirations of the Taiwanese population. After seventy-five years of isolation from mainland China, it would be surprising if the Taiwanese did not feel some degree of separate identity quite different from that in mainland Chinese provinces. Once the direct results of "U.S. imperialist aggression against China" are erased the intensity of Taiwanese separatist feeling can be measured and can be taken into account in any final settlement of Taiwan's status.

(4) Whatever the formal legal status of Taiwan ultimately becomes, there ought to be some sort of special relationship with China. Ideally Taiwan would become a province of the People's Republic. If political realities make this impossible, an acceptable alternative might be a genuinely autonomous Taiwan for the indefinite future, under nominal Chinese sovereignty; at some future date Taiwan might again merge with the mainland. Or, alternatively, although no Chinese will speak of it at this time, it is conceivable that at some future date the Chinese people and government might decide that the perpetuation of this nominal sovereignty over Taiwan was of no substantial benefit to China and that it would not be against China's vital interest to agree to Taiwanese self-determination. Even then, however, China would probably insist on certain conditions. Taiwan could not in any sense be permitted to be a threat to Chinese interests and would certainly be expected to maintain close, friendly relations with China. Taiwan would not be permitted to be a client state of any other power, specifically the United States or Japan. To China a long-term defensive alliance between the United States and Taiwan would be intolerable. Although the Japanese appear at this time to have no desire to re-establish political con-

trol over Taiwan, there is in the economic realm a natural affinity between Japan and Taiwan. This affinity is so great that an
independent Taiwan might eventually become an integral part of
a Japanese economic empire. If this occurred, the development
of a political client state relationship would be difficult to avoid.
Such a re-assertion of Japanese power and influence over Taiwan
would be as unacceptable to the Chinese as would a client state
relationship with the United States.

Again, the Chinese have not said these things; it is easy to
find evidence to counter the above argument that there may be
some degree of flexibility in the Chinese position on Taiwan. For
instance, it can be pointed out that Peking's propaganda has with
increasing vehemence branded the organized Taiwanese independent movement (TIM) as a U.S. plot designed to "perpetuate
U.S. imperialist occupation of Taiwan" by "cutting Taiwan off
from China."[172] Perhaps this line results partly from the fact that
the TIM to date has understandably directed its efforts at influencing the United States and other non-Communist governments and has ignored Peking. The current pro-U.S. orientation
of the TIM is not designed to win the favor of Peking. Peking
could conclude that if the presently identifiable TIM leaders came
to power an independent Taiwan would be no less a U.S. client
state than is the GRC. From Peking's point of view this would
almost certainly be an unacceptable solution to the Taiwan
problem.

Since any hoped-for solution that would provide the Taiwanese a substantial measure of influence in determining their future
must ultimately have the consent of China, it would be reasonable to expect that those who hope to see Taiwan remain out of
Communist hands would make a major effort to determine just
what the Chinese really feel and want, and with what intensity,
in regard to Taiwan. But one searches the public record largely in
vain for evidence of curiosity on the part of U.S. policy makers
about the middle ground between the belief that Peking's demand
for the "liberation" of Taiwan is absolute, irrevocable, and total,
and the contradictory implicit assumption of U.S. policy since the
early 1960s that if only the United States stands firm the Chinese
will ultimately be deterred from "aggression" against Taiwan and,

presumably, learn to live with something resembling the "Two Chinas" status quo.

The U.S. Government has not seriously pursued the possibility that while a rival Chinese government on Taiwan is intolerable to Peking there might be conditions under which Peking could learn to live with a Taiwan controlled by the Taiwanese. Although the Chinese have never hinted at a willingness to accept self-determination for Taiwan, it should be recognized that they have never had to face the real strength of the argument for Taiwanese separation. As long as the GRC rules, Peking need respond to no argument for such a separation because the GRC insists above all else that Taiwan belongs to China.

If, in contrast, the Taiwanese were in control, Peking would have to consider the following: Taiwan would be a quite homogeneous state with a popular government leading a population united in its determination to run its own affairs. This state would have excellent defenses, including a 100-mile-wide moat, and the will to defend itself. While insisting on defending their autonomy and right to self-determination, the Taiwanese would have every reason to develop friendly, cooperative relations with Communist China because their very existence would ultimately depend on the good will of China. An internally strong and united Taiwan which had a vigorous non-communist economy and society, and which did not welcome Chinese control, would be difficult for Communist China to digest, even if force were openly resorted to.

It should be remembered that Taiwan has been completely bypassed by the Communist revolution, and that the population has no desire for communism. Would an embittered, inherently anti-Communist Taiwan that Peking could only control forcibly really be an asset to Peking? Would this be more desirable than an independent or genuinely autonomous Taiwan that no longer claimed to be the government of China, from which the U.S. military presence was gradually but steadily phased out, and which wanted friendly, cooperative relations with Peking? It is not inconceivable that, faced with such a choice, a more mature Peking which had won its own rightful place in the world could, in time, reconcile itself to Taiwanese self-determination.

The Political Realities of Taiwan

Problems of Political Research and Analysis on Taiwan

THE AMERICAN ACADEMIC community and the U.S. Government are perhaps as well informed about the fundamental political realities of Communist China as they are about those of Taiwan. This is largely due to the different levels of interest and concern on the part of Americans. For every hour spent by scholars or government specialists trying to understand Taiwan, hundreds are devoted to mainland China. Even scholars who reside for substantial amounts of time on Taiwan are, with few exceptions, there for what they can learn about the "other" China. They study the Mandarin Chinese language and generally specialize in the fields of Chinese history, Chinese literature, or other fields relating to mainland China. Taiwan is looked upon not as an entity of value in itself but as an accessible base for studying the "real" China.[173] The review in this book of the approaches of successive U.S. administrations to the Taiwan problem suggests that at the top levels of the U.S. Government there has been very little curiosity about the internal political realities of Taiwan.

Responsible observers of the Taiwanese scene have arrived at differing assessments of the realities of Taiwanese politics. Some have reported after years of residence that they observed no visible signs of any significant interest on the part of the Taiwanese in replacing the GRC with a native Taiwanese-controlled government.[174] Others have concluded that the Taiwanese are definitely in favor of independence and are only kept from attaining this aim by GRC suppression.[175] They are likely to believe that it is so obvious that the Taiwanese want to control their own affairs that any realistic discussion of Taiwan must start from this assumption. It should be clear from such divergent conclusions about Taiwan that the political realities of the island are not readily apparent to every reasonably intelligent outside observer.

The official GRC line is that the GRC is only temporarily on Taiwan awaiting the opportune moment to return to the mainland. The mainland recovery goal, claims the GRC, is shared by all the people of Taiwan, even the 85 percent native Taiwanese majority. The native Taiwanese, it is claimed, are and feel themselves to be 100 percent Chinese; they fully accept the "legitimate" Chinese government (the GRC) and have no desire for independence. For instance, the publication, *101 Questions About Taiwan*, which is designed to explain Taiwan to foreign visitors, says,

91. Is there cooperation between the local people and those from the mainland?

There is not only goodwill and cooperation between the local population and those from the mainland; they are one people, sharing the same traditions and customs, reading and writing the same language. There is no distinction between the "Taiwanese," and the "mainlanders" as they are all Chinese, whether born on this island or in provinces on the mainland. . . .

98. Do the island-born soldiers share the enthusiasm for the recovery of the mainland?

They most certainly do, for they are also Chinese, sharing the same cherished objectives of freedom and democracy and feeling the same sort of kinship to those suffering under Communist tyranny on the mainland. They realize that Taiwan is an integral part of China and that their families would not be safe unless the Chinese Communist regime is overthrown.

It is most unlikely that any reasonably alert American student of Taiwan today accepts these claims literally. It is widely recognized in government and academic circles that these are GRC ideals and that the truth lies some distance from these official claims. Confronted with the nature of the political system on Taiwan, however, it is difficult to discern just what this distance is. The GRC has been effective in assuring that once the foreigner gets away from the official line he is on shaky ground and will have difficulty finding concrete evidence to build a case against the GRC's official claims. No public expression of Taiwanese discontent is permitted; any Taiwanese who publicly expresses political sentiments in contradiction to the official line is subject to immediate arrest. Furthermore, all Taiwanese are thoroughly indoctrinated to know what it is not permissible to say except in the company of close friends and relatives. The Taiwanese knows that he cannot in safety publicly attack Chiang Kai-shek or the notion that the GRC will recover the mainland just as the citizen of Communist China knows that he cannot publicly attack Mao Tse-tung or the desirability of Communism.

While few foreigners accept completely the official GRC claims about the Taiwanese desire to recover the mainland or Taiwanese lack of interest in self-determination, most observers have a hard time answering such questions as: "Assuming the Taiwanese do not accept the official line, what do they believe?" "How strong is the Taiwanese sentiment in favor of independence?" "How deep is their dislike for the GRC?"

Without well-documented answers to these questions it is difficult to see how an instinctively pro-GRC U.S. policy maker could be expected to seriously contemplate switching to a policy based on the interests of the native Taiwanese as opposed to the present policy of support for the Mainlander-dominated GRC. Much of American official opinion rests in uncertainty somewhere between the belief that the Taiwanese have minor complaints about the system, similar to those that any people would have about their government, and the belief that the Taiwanese would overthrow the GRC at the first opportunity and establish an independent state.

The GRC has successfully kept the American assessment of

the true state of Taiwanese opinion in this fog. Of great benefit to the GRC in this effort is the fact that many Americans are ideologically inclined to be friendly to the GRC. These people can point to a vast amount of published data to defend their favorable inclinations toward "Free China." Those who are critical of the GRC must dig and scrape for supporting data that is sufficiently concrete to convince the GRC's committed friends that they should question their long-standing support for "Free China."

The thinking of the Mainlanders is no less difficult to probe than that of the Taiwanese. The Mainlanders are aware that the political system of the GRC depends on unquestioned adherence to the notion that the GRC is the sole legitimate government of China and that the government is only temporarily in Taiwan awaiting the inevitable recovery of the mainland. Under the present system, 1,404 of 1,430 national assemblymen (who elect the president) represent the mainland provinces; they were elected in 1947 and are in office today only because new elections have been suspended for the duration of the "Communist rebellion" (i.e., until the GRC recovers the mainland). New elections based only on Taiwan would without question lead to Taiwanese majorities.

In the Legislative Yuan, the law-making body, 434 of the 440 members[176] were elected to represent the mainland provinces in 1948. If the supporters of the GRC were to admit that the GRC is not really the government of all China, they would be unable to rationalize the perpetuation of a government dependent on the indefinite suspension of elections in order to maintain in office representatives elected from territories the government hasn't controlled for over twenty years.

Aside from the national assemblymen and legislators, the Mainlanders with the greatest stake in perpetuating the present system include those in the central government bureaucracies (for instance, the Commission for Tibetan Affairs), military officers (although a number of Taiwanese have reached the rank of major, there are very few above that; one source reports that there were 86 Taiwanese among 14,000 majors in 1969[177]), those employed by the government corporations (which are staffed primarily by Mainlanders and which have been accused even by friendly Americans of thwarting the development of free enterprise, which is primarily a Taiwanese activity), and school teachers (particularly those who teach Chinese-oriented subjects such as the Mandarin language and Chinese history).

If the government on Taiwan ceased to consider itself the government of all China, the jobs of all these people might be in jeopardy. These people, who constitute the institutionalized political elite on Taiwan, therefore have important reasons for supporting the official myth of mainland recovery. They cannot be expected to admit to outsiders or perhaps in some cases even to themselves that the GRC is not going to retake the mainland.

Because of the stake the Mainlanders have in the sanctity of the official myths, they can easily rationalize that the omnipresent and omnipotent security system designed to ferret out any indication of organized Taiwanese opposition is essential to the "sacred national interest" of China. Many of them do not like martial law but realize it is necessary to the "national interest" for the duration of the "Communist rebellion." They hasten to explain, of course, that martial law is a temporary measure to meet the current extraordinary circumstances that have existed since 1949. They assure the foreign friend that as soon as the mainland is recovered martial law will be abolished and elections above the local level, along with other manifestations of democracy guaranteed in the GRC's 1947 constitution, will be restored.

Political Background (1945 to the Present)

During World War II the Allied powers agreed that Taiwan should be returned to China. The most formal pledge to this effect was in the Cairo Declaration of December 1943. As Taiwanese nationalists point out, the Taiwanese were in no way consulted about this. However, given the circumstances at the time, it was reasonable for the Allies to make this pledge. Taiwan did have an ethnic Chinese population, and it had been taken over by Japan as the spoils of war against the wishes of the Taiwanese people in 1895. Available information about Taiwan indicated that Japanese rule had been oppressive and that the Taiwanese people were far from content with their lot under the Japanese.[178]

The initial reaction to Chinese control following Japan's surrender indicated that the decision at Cairo had been well-founded. The Taiwanese gave every indication of being happy to be out from under Japanese control; Mandarin language schools sprouted and thousands of Taiwanese voluntarily enrolled to learn the language of their Chinese compatriots. Even active Taiwanese nationalists admit today that on the whole the Taiwanese originally welcomed the Nationalist administration.[179]

The Nationalist administration that was set up in 1945 was corrupt and oppressive.[180] Even writers who were favorably inclined toward Chiang's government describe it as exemplifying the worst features of the Nationalist administration in its final years on the mainland.[181] Tension soon developed between the Taiwanese and the Mainlander authorities. By February 1947 this tension was at a high pitch, and a minor incident of police brutality set off the "2-28 (February 28) Incident."[182] Taiwanese took over almost complete control of the island, but they did not demand independence. Instead, their demands were for reform of the administration of Governor Ch'en Yi.[183] An ad hoc Taiwanese council ("Settlement Committee") was established and prepared a reform program for submission to Ch'en Yi. Ch'en agreed to have the program presented to him on March 10 and promised that no more government troops would be sent to Taiwan.

However, Ch'en had secretly communicated with Nanking and requested Chiang to send troops to Taiwan to strengthen his hand. The troops landed on March 8. The council was immediately disbanded and the Nationalists rounded up Taiwanese suspected of having been involved in the revolt, including a substantial proportion of the Taiwanese elite. There are no precise figures on the number executed; some Taiwanese estimate 10,000 to 20,000, while foreigners on Taiwan at the time estimated at least 5,000.[184]

On Taiwan one frequently meets Taiwanese who had relatives or friends who were executed in the roundup following the "2-28 Incident." Taiwanese nationalists today claim that "2-28" was the prime catalyst in causing Taiwanese activists to move from advocacy of reform of the GRC administration to advocacy of Taiwanese independence.

The maladministration of Governor Ch'en Yi was publicly condemned by Chiang Kai-shek in mid-1950, at which time Ch'en was executed for his "crimes" in Taiwan from 1945 to 1947.[185] But this belated execution did not convince the Taiwanese that Chiang had really executed Ch'en for his misdeeds on Taiwan. Chiang had removed Ch'en from the governorship in late March 1947 as a direct consequence of the February incident, but instead of punishing him then Chiang had rewarded him by making him a senior advisor and then governor of Chekiang (Chiang's own home province), a province with a larger area and population than Taiwan. In fact, Chiang did not decide to punish Ch'en until the latter was discovered to be in contact with the Communists, presumably with the idea of making a deal with them.[186] To many Taiwanese today Chiang's punishment of Ch'en immediately after the Chiang government had fled from the mainland to Taiwan was not a genuine expression of sorrow at Ch'en's misdeeds in Taiwan, but a cynical attempt to curry favor with the Taiwanese.

After the Communist victory on the mainland and the flight of the GRC to Taiwan, Taiwan settled into the pattern that has continued to the present. From the time of Chiang's arrival the foundation of the political system has been unquestioned adherence to the mainland recovery theme and total suppression of all Taiwanese opposition sentiment. As early as February 1950, Chiang Kai-shek was promising to counterattack the mainland and execute Mao Tse-tung.[187] Even today, with Chiang Kai-shek progressively transferring power to his son Chiang Ching-kuo, the mainland recovery theme remains as essential as ever to the continued existence of GRC rule on Taiwan.

In April 1970 Chiang Ching-kuo visited the United States and went out of his way to present a moderate and reasonable image, but he could not allow any doubts about the mainland recovery theme. Chiang said in a speech on April 24 in New York:

. . . Free China is not only an obstacle to Communist aggression but also an alternative to Chinese Communism itself and to the Peking regime's possession of the Chinese mainland. In your country there are those who question the realism of the Republic of China's return to the mainland. For our part, we question the realism of a failure to return. If we do not, and if the Communist system is clamped down on the Chinese people in perpetuity, there will be no peace in Asia or the world.

Let me speak frankly. The Chinese Communists cannot possibly survive, unless they are given a new lease of life by the free world, of which the United States is the leader. The Peiping regime has held the mainland for two decades and has been close to collapse on more than one occasion.[188]

On April 26, Chiang Ching-kuo told 300 overseas Chinese businessmen in Los Angeles that the return to the mainland "is not very far off and a very sure thing."[189]

Since 1950 Taiwan has made substantial economic progress although Taiwanese point out endlessly that the economic advance has been made upon a solid foundation built by the Japanese. By World War II Taiwan was far ahead of any area of mainland China in transportation, electrification, education, industrial and agricultural production, and public order. That the GRC has been able to build on this foundation is to its credit, but it is hardly in a position to take the credit for all of Taiwan's current economic development. Furthermore, Taiwan has received over $1.5 billion in U.S. economic aid since 1950 (and $2,522,600,000 in military aid, of which $2,490,400,000 was in grants).[190] The Taiwanese point out that even the vaunted land reform carried out on Taiwan in the 1950s was designed at least in part to damage the political power base of the Taiwanese landlords, who were perhaps the leading element in the native Taiwanese political elite. Taiwanese note that although Chiang was never willing to institute land reform on the mainland where much of his support came from landlords, he did not hesitate to institute it on Taiwan where the land-owning class was among his strongest potential opponents.

If the only standard by which the future of Taiwan should

be judged were economic, the future would appear relatively bright in comparison with most other developing Asian countries. There are dark spots to be sure, and many Taiwanese are convinced that had it not been for the burden of the Nationalist bureaucracy, military and state-run segment of the economy (which the Taiwanese see as operated primarily for the benefit of the Mainlanders in the government), the economy today would be well ahead of its present state, given the economic infrastructure inherited from Japan. But, generally speaking, the economic outlook for Taiwan is reasonably bright. The island's future problems are overwhelmingly political.

It is argued in this book that the GRC political system depends on the maintenance of the "myth" of mainland recovery. Students of comparative politics may question that a system which has its share of successes in the economic sphere and which has been able to maintain order and stability could be based on nothing more than a myth. Surely, these students may contend, there must be other elements within the political structure which contribute to the persistence of the system.

In a sense, the contention is well founded. The Taiwanese do receive an adequate share of the economic rewards, and in education, local politics, the fine arts, entertainment, and other fields the degree of discrimination against them is by no means intolerable. When it is argued here that the GRC political system depends on the recovery myth, what is meant is that the central government (the so-called government of China), with its present Mainlander leaders, its overgrown bureaucracy and army, its fundamental mainland-oriented goals, and its mainland-oriented symbols—and these are the characteristic attributes of the GRC —depends on the myth.

If the myth were eliminated, the society need not fall into chaos, except as a result of serious conflict between the old (Mainlander) and the new (Taiwanese) ruling groups. (As the author points out elsewhere, this is a possibility which those concerned with Taiwan's future must take into account.) What would happen to the system if the myth were removed would be that the raison d'etre of the GRC would disappear and with it the sole rationale for continued suppression of the natural development of a representative, Taiwanese-controlled government.

In other words, at least in comparison with most developing Asian nations, the present system meets many of the demands, whether articulated or not, of the population. What it fundamentally fails to meet are (1) the long-range aspirations of the great majority of the population regarding the fundamental political and legal status of Taiwan and (2) the inherent desire on the part of the Taiwanese educated elite for an effective voice in their own government.

For the Taiwanese who avoids politics completely, the system is not unbearably oppressive. It is only to the extent that the Taiwanese concerns himself with politics that he feels himself living under an intolerable system. He knows that it is nothing but force or the threat of force that keeps him from expressing his genuine desires for the political future of Taiwan and prevents him from meaningful involvement in the politics of the island. Most Taiwanese have shown that they can tolerate the GRC system, at least for the present, but only to the extent that they direct their thoughts and energies elsewhere than to the fundamental political problems of Taiwan.

Given the nature of GRC security controls, it is understandable that there is no effectively organized Taiwanese independence movement on Taiwan. The movement, insofar as it is organized, is an exile phenomenon. It is centered in Japan and the United States and much of its energy is expended in persuading the governments and peoples of those two countries to support Taiwanese independence. The movement enjoys the support of a substantial number of Taiwanese abroad.[191] Few if any of its supporters who have left Taiwan since 1949 had made any public commitment to Taiwanese independence before going abroad—otherwise they would not have been allowed to leave. The GRC contends that all of them were pure and loyal GRC supporters while on Taiwan and that they have been corrupted since leaving the motherland.

In a speech to some 250 visiting journalists of the International Press Institute on May 23, 1970, Chiang Kai-shek said:

In fact, the so-called "Formosan Independence Movement" has no followers in Taiwan. They are only a handful of professional students abroad lured by others to work hand in glove with the Communists and become "Communist Formosan Independents." They are actually financed by the Maoists while overtly being attacked by them.[192]

The Taiwanese, on the other hand, argue that they felt the same way at home as they do abroad, but that they knew they had to keep their opinions to themselves while on Taiwan. There is probably some truth to both points of view. There is no doubt that many Taiwanese on Taiwan do actively desire independence, but some have very poorly formulated political opinions before they come under the influence of the organized movement abroad. Lung-chu Ch'en, co-author of pro-independence *Formosa, China, and the United Nations,* is quoted on the book jacket as admitting that when he first arrived in the United States as a graduate student he described himself as a citizen of "Free China." But it is obvious that in his mind the latent aspiration for Taiwanese separatism was just below the surface, and he was immediately responsive to the organized appeal of the Taiwanese independence movement (TIM).

Supporting the TIM while abroad makes it impossible for a Taiwanese to return to Taiwan in safety, unless he formally repents, in which case the GRC will allow him to return. Most of those who actively participate in the movement expect to remain abroad for as long as the present political situation continues on Taiwan—that is, until the present GRC rule is terminated. They say that if Taiwan had a representative, popular government they would return.[193] In this respect they are different from the Mainlanders studying abroad, few of whom have any intention of returning to live on Taiwan. In all, over 90 percent of the students who come to the United States remain permanently.[194] In Taiwan one rarely talks to a Mainlander or Taiwanese student who would not like to study abroad, but due to the tremendous competition only some 2,000 of the best students actually make it each year. The fact that out of this group less than

10 percent return to Taiwan means that the island is being drained of its best talent.

On the part of the Mainlanders, who in many cases admit that their primary interest is simply to get out of Taiwan, which they do not feel is their home, which they do not like, and which they expect will eventually either be taken over by the Taiwanese or given to Communist China, the unwillingness to return is related primarily to personal interests. With the Taiwanese, on the other hand, the lack of interest in returning is directly related to their dislike of the present regime.

Although there is no effective organized movement for Taiwanese independence on Taiwan, certain individuals have from time to time undertaken significant pro-independence actions. The most notable case was probably that of Professor P'eng Ming-min in September 1964. P'eng was chairman of the Department of Political Science at National Taiwan University at the time, and was apparently trusted by the GRC. In 1963 Chiang Kai-shek had honored him as one of ten "outstanding young people," and in 1961 P'eng had been sent to the United Nations as a member of the GRC delegation, a unique opportunity for a Taiwanese. In 1964 P'eng and two assistants composed a "Declaration of Taiwanese Independence" and gave it to a printer whom they presumably trusted, but the printer informed the police and P'eng and his two associates were arrested. Although the document never saw the light of day on Taiwan, the manuscript was smuggled abroad and it is now accepted as a basic document of the TIM abroad.

Due partly to foreign, including American, pressure P'eng was given a light sentence of eight years.[195] After he signed a confession admitting his "wrong-doings" he was released from prison, after serving only thirteen months, and put under police surveillance. The GRC's leniency in P'eng's case was perhaps facilitated by his earlier surface collaboration with the government and the government's belief that a P'eng who had admitted his errors was better than a martyred P'eng in jail.

In January 1970 P'eng somehow managed to escape the island to exile in Sweden; he later entered the United States and is now at the University of Michigan. The reception of this news by the Taiwanese abroad indicates that P'eng's future as a TIM leader is very promising. P'eng's 1964 effort, though seemingly amateurish from a tactical point of view, gave him much prestige among the Taiwanese. Few Taiwanese say they disagree with P'eng's goals, although a number admit that he was foolish to do such a thing and get caught at it.[196] P'eng, who holds a law degree from McGill University in Canada and a doctorate from the University of Paris, has developed into the most promising and respected Taiwanese political leader of the post-war era—an era in which the GRC has been careful to avoid allowing any Taiwanese to establish a charismatic image or attain much real political power.

P'eng's prestige among Taiwanese is greater than was that of Thomas Liao (Liao Wen-i), who was the leader of the exiled TIM from 1950 to 1965. Liao left Taiwan in the wake of the February 1947 incident and had to some extent lost touch with the internal situation. In 1965 Liao defected to the GRC and returned to Taiwan, largely, he said, to see his aged mother. Liao's true motives are not known, but it seems unlikely that he suddenly and sincerely changed his views about the fundamental questions relating to Taiwan's future.[197]

If P'eng survives the end of the GRC, he stands an excellent chance of becoming a future leader of Taiwan. Other potential leaders exist but few of them have island-wide political reputations today. Taipei mayor Kao Yu-shu is an exception. Kao, although widely believed to be in favor of increased Taiwanization of the government, has worked within the system, which has meant constant compromise with the GRC. He therefore lacks P'eng's reputation for idealistic commitment to the Taiwanese cause and is considered to be something of a political opportunist.

There are no Taiwanese, other than a handful of obvious puppets, in high positions in the GRC. Even the governor is a Mainlander appointed by Chiang Kai-shek because provincial gubernatorial elections, like central government elections, have been suspended for the duration of the present "extraordinary circumstances."

Taiwanese Thinking

When an unfamiliar foreigner approaches a Taiwanese on Taiwan and attempts to engage him in discussion of the island's fundamental political issues, the Taiwanese is likely to be cautious. In talking with the author, most Taiwanese presented an initial pose of support for the official myths of the GRC. Further probing of those with whom additional contact was established enabled the author to divide them into two groups:

(1) Those who either because of genuine lack of interest in politics or fear of any sort of political controversy eschewed political discussion. This group, after an initial expression of support for the GRC, claimed no further interest in politics. None of these people maintained beyond the initial formalities that they genuinely believed any of the pillars of the GRC myth: that the GRC is the legitimate government of China, that it will recover the mainland, or that it is the popular choice of the people of Taiwan. Instead, they either claimed they were not interested in such matters or said they preferred not to discuss them.

(2) Those who expressed an interest in political questions including the future of Taiwan. All of these opposed the GRC and favored eventual Taiwanese control. Although in agreement on these fundamental questions, they differed considerably about tactics. Almost none favored an early violent revolution, primarily because they felt it could not succeed without unacceptable costs. Most of them also felt that, even if successful, a revolution would not be desirable. They preferred to see an evolutionary change within a reasonably short period of time, during which they could win over the allegiance of the Mainlanders on Taiwan to an independent Taiwanese government, rather than risk a violent revolution which might cause the KMT to attempt to make a deal to turn the island over to Peking.

The second group felt that the eventual turnover of power to the Taiwanese would probably be spurred by external events rather than internal ones and almost invariably held that the trigger most likely to set the process in motion would be withdrawal of U.S. support from the GRC. Without this support, they felt, the

GRC's internal and external prestige would collapse. Once this happened the Mainlanders would become increasingly subject to pressures for a gradual transfer of power to the Taiwanese, provided the Mainlanders were assured of fair treatment.

The fundamental belief of these Taiwanese concerning Mainlander resistance to Taiwanization was that the Mainlanders know their entire system rests on a fictitious foundation and that once this is publicly acknowledged inside and outside of Taiwan the entire GRC structure will begin to crumble. These Taiwanese reasoned that this must happen within the next decade or two, and that since it is inevitable they would be foolish to risk a premature revolt that might either be successfully suppressed by the GRC or lead to a KMT deal with Peking.

Of most interest to the author as a result of his conversations with Taiwanese was that no Taiwanese—not even one—maintained beyond an initial cautious pose that he sincerely believed the fundamental myths of the GRC. It would not be going too far to say that to all of those in at least the second group the notion that any educated Taiwanese could literally believe the official mainland-oriented claims of the GRC was ludicrous. This was true even of Taiwanese businessmen who have profited greatly under GRC rule and who are. conservative in regard to anti-GRC tactics that might threaten the stability essential to their continued prosperity.

Educated Taiwanese simply assume that at least the politically alert segment of the Taiwanese population is united in desiring eventual Taiwanese control over the island. They assume this fact is not readily apparent to non-Taiwanese for the sole reason that the GRC has vigorously suppressed open Taiwanese expressions of discontent. They maintain that although uneducated Taiwanese might not have well-formulated political aspirations, even the peasantry has a latent desire for Taiwanese separatism, and that this desire would surface immediately once it became permissible for Taiwanese leaders to openly attack the myths that maintain GRC rule.

It is difficult to assess the degree to which the sample of Taiwanese opinion explored by the author might be representative. It obviously included only a small segment of the educated

elite, and it is doubtful if the majority of the Taiwanese population has thought things out to the same extent. Unquestionably,
less educated Taiwanese would have less well-formulated criticisms
of the GRC and less clear opinions about what they would like
to see happen to Taiwan in the future. But it is not unlikely that
the peasants and the less educated would have latent tendencies
similar to those more fully developed among the elite. This appears to be the usual pattern in colonial situations. The first to
formulate specific criticisms of the system are the intellectuals; once
they break the theoretical ground and the situation allows, latent
nationalist or separatist tendencies can be readily brought to the
surface by vigorous leadership.

Whatever the peasants think now will not, in any case, determine the future of Taiwan. Any conceivable Taiwanese political
leadership that might emerge in the foreseeable future would almost certainly come from the educated elite. These people appear
to be convinced of the justice of ultimate Taiwanese control of
the island and intellectually united in rejection of the fundamental
premises of the GRC.

But, supporters of the current U.S. commitment to the GRC
might ask, if there is a coherent intellectual unity (even among
the small minority of politically alert and active members of the
Taiwanese elite) in favor of replacing the GRC with an independent Taiwan, how is it that so many U.S. officials and others can
live on Taiwan for years and observe no strong manifestations of
serious Taiwanese discontent with the system?

The Taiwanese community can be divided into three political categories: (1) a vast majority who are politically inert; (2)
a minority who are politically aware but willing to wait rather
than risk a violent, revolutionary change, believing that, provided
Taiwan stays out of Communist Chinese hands, control will
eventually fall to the Taiwanese through attrition of the Mainlander leadership; and (3) a very small number who are willing
to take action under present circumstances. Most of the last are
in prison.[198]

Chinese Nationalist indoctrination over the last twenty-five
years has convinced all except the third group that they should
not attempt to oppose the system, though it has not made rele-

vant to any significant number of Taiwanese the fundamental mainland-oriented goals of the GRC (except, as Taiwanese wags point out, that a successful "counterattack" would at least have the virtue of ridding Taiwan of the Mainlanders).

The Taiwanese have been a subject people since 1895. They are accustomed to submitting to outside authority. There should be no reason, it can be argued, to expect them to show a greater willingness to confront the system than was the case with the colonial people of other countries as long as the colonial regimes remained solidly in control. A Taiwanese who expressed his honest views about the mainland recovery theme or the justice of Taiwanese self-determination would be in a more dangerous situation than would an anti-British Indian nationalist in the 1920s and 1930s.

Americans can by analogy with the experience of numerous colonies since World War II reason that the native populations of Angola, Mozambique, or even the blacks of South Africa must have now or will surely develop a strong desire for self-determination. But American observers looking at Taiwan see the native Taiwanese as ethnic Chinese, with largely the same history, culture, and language. The surface differences between Taiwanese and Mainlanders are hard for Americans to detect.

The desire for Taiwanese separation is apparent to non-Taiwanese only in private conversation with politically interested members of the Taiwanese elite. Given the interest of U.S. academic students in the "other" China and the demands on U.S. officials who have official dealings almost exclusively with the Mainlanders of the GRC, it is not surprising that the Taiwanese separatist aspiration is often overlooked. The tendency to downgrade Taiwanese desires is undoubtedly strengthened if the American has an ideological commitment against Communist China with a corresponding reaction in favor of "Free China."

An important question for Taiwan's future is the attitude of the Taiwanese majority toward the individual Mainlanders in their midst. This is not easy to assess. There is some bitterness, but its intensity is difficult to measure because open discussion of Taiwanese-Mainlander conflict is suppressed. Many Mainlanders probably feel they are sitting atop a cauldron and that once they give an inch they will be consumed by the boiling wrath of twenty-five years of accumulated Taiwanese bitterness. The Mainlanders frequently defend their regime in private conversation by saying they are afraid they would be "driven into the sea" by an independent Taiwanese regime.

The Taiwanese readily admit that they would be better off if the Mainlanders had never come; some say they hope the United States or other countries will accept many Mainlanders as immigrants once the final demise of the GRC occurs. However, responsible Taiwanese (and this includes for all practical purposes all of those whose views formed the basis of the conclusions here) are convinced that the chances for a future Taiwan that is prosperous, stable, and able to maintain its independence from mainland China will be maximized if the Taiwanese accept the Mainlanders on a basis of equality. They philosophize that "We are all Taiwanese now; the only difference is that the present Mainlanders have just arrived while our ancestors have been here for centuries." Responsible Taiwanese claim that they feel little bitterness toward individual Mainlanders in their midst and that it is only the present political system that they find intolerable.

These views represent current high-minded Taiwanese ideals. In any actual future situation involving a transfer of power from the Mainlanders to the Taiwanese, there would undoubtedly be a release of emotions on both sides. The degree to which moderates on both sides would be able to keep these emotions in check is difficult to assess, but would be an important factor in the chances for a non-violent transfer of power and a peaceful future.

The more cautious Taiwanese argue that it is in the Taiwanese interest to put up with GRC rule for a while longer because the greater the number of older Mainlander leaders and officials who die, the less there will be of die-hard resistance to Taiwanese control once it becomes clear that the final demise of the GRC is about to occur. However, the Taiwanese also argue that justice demands an early elimination of the GRC's dictatorial rule and the establishment of a representative and democratic (i.e., Taiwanese-controlled) government on Taiwan.

Politically interested Taiwanese thus face conflicting pressures: to attempt on the one hand to take control as soon as possible, and on the other to be cautious and let time work in their interest. Many Taiwanese resolve this conflict in their own minds by placing responsibility on the United States. They say the crucial factor in destroying the myth upon which GRC rule rests will be the withdrawal of U.S. support for it. Once the United States publicly proclaims that the GRC has no right to speak for China after all, the GRC will soon collapse.

These Taiwanese argue that with an effort that would be minimal in comparison with what the United States already has invested in the GRC, the United States could prevent Mainlander extremists from turning the island over to Peking. If only the United States would make clear to the Mainlanders that their political never-never land was about to end, say these Taiwanese, most Mainlanders could resign themselves to life under a democratic Taiwanese-controlled Taiwan—and the political aims of those who could not do so should be ignored anyway.

It is sometimes argued that while the Taiwanese hope for an end to Nationalist rule, they are vague about whether they would prefer to see it replaced by an independent Taiwanese government or by reversion to Communist China.[199] This seems inconsistent with the entire thrust of Taiwanese thinking as observable in the 1960s. They want independence and they see the risk of possible Communist Chinese control as the greatest threat to the ultimate realization of this dream. But Peking is largely an unknown quantity. The Taiwanese realize that Peking presently demands control over Taiwan, but they have a vague feeling that if only Mao knew that the Taiwanese really want independence and would be willing to fight for it he would be reasonable enough to let them have it. They feel that for mainland China Mao is probably an improvement over the Chiang regime of the 1940s. This is undoubtedly partly a reaction to their own predicament, but they cite historical evidence for their view: Chiang, they say, was driven out of China by a Chinese people desperate enough to give his Communist challengers a chance.

A few Taiwanese cited Napal and Burma as evidence that small, reasonably friendly countries would not be threatened by China and said they believed Taiwan could attain a similar position. This interest in a neutral status is in conflict with the often expressed hope of most Taiwanese that for some time to come Taiwan can continue to enjoy U.S. protection. It appears that most would not want to put themselves at China's mercy in the near future, although it is accepted as axiomatic that some day Taiwan will have to come to terms with China and that the terms must be reasonably friendly if Taiwan is to expect China to respect her independence.

In truth, the Taiwanese have very little basis for estimating future Chinese Communist attitudes toward them. Communist materials are unavailable on Taiwan to any but specially cleared GRC observers of Communist China, and these are almost exclusively Mainlanders. Few Taiwanese have ever seen any Chinese Communist statements except in the context the GRC media have chosen to present them.

The attitude of a small minority of Taiwanese was perhaps indicated by a young man who went to the United States to study. The first thing he did after arriving at his campus was to rush to the library and check out the Peking *People's Daily*. He had heard so much GRC propaganda against the Communist regime that he felt the regime must be good. The content of the paper shocked him. He said to himself, "This is even worse than what is in the GRC papers." He rapidly lost his interest in reading the *People's Daily*. This experience convinced him even more that the Taiwanese should run their own affairs and avoid control by either Chinese regime.

Mainlander Thinking

The thinking of the native Taiwanese with regard to Taiwan's future is of obvious relevance to the future of the island, but the thinking of the Mainlanders in their midst may be just as important. The Mainlanders realize that the continued existence of their system depends on unswerving adherence to the mainland recovery theme. When one first discusses political questions with a Mainlander, in the government or out, the Mainlander will almost certainly express support for the official GRC line. He will insist that mainland recovery is only a matter of time and that the Taiwanese are Chinese and do not, nor could they ever, desire to become independent from China.

The author's contacts with Mainlanders were at least as close as those with Taiwanese during his five years on Taiwan. The only conclusion possible from these contacts was that there are few, if any, Mainlanders who really believe either of these propositions. In the majority of cases, the Mainlanders can be led to admit this by questions which do not show disrespect for what they hold dear.

One does not begin a political discussion with a Mainlander by proclaiming, "I think Chiang Kai-shek is an isolated old man who is out of touch with reality. What do you think?" or "Taiwan should obviously be governed by the Taiwanese majority. Don't you think so?" After the initial formalities, which should perhaps involve praise for some of the genuine cultural or economic achievements of GRC rule on Taiwan, it is more prudent to say something to this effect: "I think and certainly hope that the GRC can recover the mainland from the Communists, but I wonder if this can actually be done. If not, what do you think will become of Taiwan?"

If political questions are raised at the proper time and after an appropriate degree of deference to GRC or at least to Chinese beliefs, the majority of Mainlanders, even those in the government, can be maneuvered in a polite and unaggressive manner into discussing the future of Taiwan in more or less realistic terms. This does not require that the Mainlanders explicitly state that they know the mainland recovery theme is a futile myth.

The prime characteristic of the Mainlanders' political thinking is doubt about their future. In the face of this doubt they clearly hope that their present relatively secure positions can be maintained as long as possible, and this requires loyalty to the GRC and its official myths. Almost without exception they recognize the difficulties involved in recovering the mainland and realize that if the mainland is not recovered Taiwan must ultimately undergo some fundamental change in status that will be detrimental to the present ruling minority.

The ideal way out of their present dilemma would still be to reinstate the GRC on the mainland. Although they realize the chances of this are extremely remote, they continue to grasp at straws. For instance, the Chinese Communist Great Leap Forward and Cultural Revolution periods raised what appeared to be a genuine (though very small) degree of hope that the Communist regime might collapse from within, thereby allowing the GRC to play a role in replacing it. Likewise, the Vietnam conflict, at least in the first couple of years after the major U.S. buildup began in 1965, caused much speculation in GRC circles that the Communist Chinese would intervene, thereby triggering a war between the United States and Communist China. This, the speculation ran, could end in the destruction of the Communist regime and an opportunity for the GRC to return.

The talk along these lines should not be confused with genuine confidence. Nevertheless, any remote prospect for the collapse of the Peking regime has been sufficient to keep up a slight degree of hope in an essentially hopeless situation and has provided a rationale for continuing adherence to the official line with its utility in maintaining inviolate the present system on Taiwan.

The Mainlanders realize that if the GRC does not recover the mainland, Taiwan must eventually be turned over to Communist China or become independent. Since no public discussion of this choice is permitted, it is difficult to learn which alternative they prefer, even assuming they allow themselves to think about it enough to have a preference. Mainlanders with close connections to the GRC leadership have been known to say that the Taiwanese will certainly eventually take over the island, but warn that the United States should not try to expedite this inevitable process. Other Mainlanders have vehemently denied that Taiwan will ever be allowed to become independent and have said that if they had to choose they would rather see the island turned over to Peking. Some have said that if Communist China ever adopted a more moderate ("revisionist") type of communism, the GRC could readily be absorbed into it.

Among the older Mainlanders, particularly those who held responsible government positions before the GRC fled to Taiwan, the tendency to deny that Taiwan can ever become independent is stronger than among young Mainlanders.

In talking with younger Mainlanders, it becomes apparent that although ideally they would still like to see the GRC successful in retaking the mainland, most doubt quite openly in private conversation that this will ever be done. Many of them readily acknowledge that the Taiwanese have a strong claim to control over their own island and say that if the Taiwanese took over they would not find it impossible to accommodate to Taiwanese rule.

However, almost without exception, the reaction of the younger, educated Mainlanders to their uncertain future on Taiwan is to desire to get out of Taiwan for good. Those who can leave and settle in the United States or elsewhere are considered the lucky ones. Once a Mainlander student gets his visa to study abroad his friends and family often assume that he will never return to Taiwan to live. This is true whether his family holds a high position in the GRC or has no visible connection with it. A vigorously pro-GRC general told the author that two of his five children were already in the United States and he hoped that the others would get there after they graduated from college. He said he considered this a kind of "insurance"; that is, if and when the GRC collapses, he and the remainder of his family will hopefully be able to emigrate to the United States as relatives of U.S. citizens. In fact, a very large number of GRC officials, generals, and legislators have children resident in the United States, and there can be little question that they consider this a kind of "insurance." According to one estimate, the members of the GRC cabinet some years ago had, collectively, more children in the United States than in Taiwan.[200]

Although the official GRC line totally denies the existence of Taiwanese separatist feeling, this feeling obviously is seen by Mainlanders as the primary threat to the present status of the GRC. It would not be going too far to say that for a substantial segment of GRC officialdom there is an absolute obsession with the fear of a Taiwanese takeover. Public reference to Taiwanese independence activities is avoided whenever possible; when it cannot be avoided the activities are invariably branded as Communist. (This is in contrast to Peking's propaganda which brands the TIM as a tool of the U.S. "imperialists" or Japanese "reactionaries.") When Chiang Ching-kuo was in the United States in April 1970, two Taiwanese nationalists attempted to assassinate him. The official KMT newspaper, the *Central Daily News* (April 26, 1970), made no reference to the fact that the attempted assassins were Taiwanese and referred to them only as "Communist agents," which they clearly were not.[201]

Most Mainlanders, including almost all under thirty-five, could probably resign themselves to living in an independent Taiwan. On the other hand, they consider it possible that the GRC leadership after Chiang Kai-shek's death might make a deal with the post-Mao leadership of Communist China. They would not welcome this prospect, but a substantial number of them say they could live with the idea of returning to a communist China provided it had a more moderate style of communism. The Mainlanders have a very strong sense of history, a result of the Chinese tradition, and they appear genuinely to feel that what they consider the excesses of the current Maoist regime must give way eventually to a more moderate system, even if it continues to call itself communist. They have a real faith that whatever the mainland regime calls itself, Chinese good sense will ultimately overcome Maoist ideological dogmatism.

Most Mainlanders—especially the young—have given at least some thought to the two possible future alternatives for Taiwan (independence or reversion to China) and feel today that although neither would be desirable, depending on future circumstances they could go either way. The prevailing attitude is that the future will be determined by factors beyond their control. Today, they can do little more than put off the inevitable day of reckoning by supporting the myths upon which the continued existence of the GRC depends.

Old Assumptions and New Realities

SINCE THE END OF THE KOREAN WAR, the rationale behind continued U.S. support of the GRC claim to be the legitimate government of all China has rested largely on three assumptions:

First, that the Peking regime was hostile to the United States and that any attempt to establish normal relations with it would therefore be rebuffed. There was no compelling reason, then, for the United States to abandon the GRC since such a step would have quite unpredictable consequences.

Second, that there remained at least a chance, however remote, that the Communist regime might collapse, thus allowing the non-communist, "free" alternative government on Taiwan to play a role on the mainland favorable to American political interests in the Far East.

Third, that while the Taiwanese did, admittedly, have minor grievances against their government, the GRC was not so oppressive that the United States should decide on moral grounds to reduce its vigorous support of the "Free Chinese" regime.

The first of these assumptions, the United States' belief that Communist China was implacably hostile, continued without significant questioning through the 1960s. The U.S. Government is now, however, trying to improve relations with Peking. Since Peking's long-standing political aims in regard to Asia in general and Taiwan in particular do not appear to have changed fundamentally, it is clear that what has changed most has been the attitude in Washington. For, while during the 1950s and 1960s the United States acted on the premise that an isolated China would benefit the "Free World", the United States today has apparently come to feel that China cannot be forever in quarantine and that it would be desirable for China to be readmitted to the family of nations.

The second assumption—that the GRC had some chance of eventually returning to political power on the mainland—has received no serious consideration by any administration since 1960. Even Eisenhower and Dulles probably did not entertain more than a minimal belief in this optimistic notion. Why, then, did the Eisenhower administration attempt to keep alive the GRC's aspirations to return to the mainland? In all likelihood the administration did in fact hold out some hope, however remote, that the government in Peking would collapse and that it could be replaced by the GRC. This wishful thinking was vital to the GRC, and the United States apparently saw no clear-cut advantage in abandoning the GRC. Thus the United States found itself stuck with full-scale support of a mythological GRC aspiration which the United States really believed to be only a highly desirable but remote hope.

This hope became even dimmer as the years passed. The contradiction between the established policy and the American policy makers' evolving assumptions about the realities of the China/Taiwan situation became increasingly evident. Yet, the policy persisted. It was not until late 1970, during the debates over the admission of Communist China to membership in the United Nations, that international pressures brought the United States to the realization that its China policy must be revised.

The third assumption underlying the old China policy—that the GRC political system was sufficiently responsive to its constituents to merit the moral support as well as the strategic military support of the United States—does not appear even now to have received the serious attention at the policy-making level that someone who knows Taiwan would expect. The nature of GRC political controls is not the kind of question that presidents and secretaries of state devote a lot of specialized attention to.

It would be quite understandable if this uncomfortable topic were swept under the rug in high-level discussion of China/Taiwan policy. In all probability, faring equally badly would be the question of the political aspirations of the Taiwanese people themselves. In comparison with such broad policy matters as the U.S. position on Chinese representation in the United Nations or the credibility of U.S. defensive commitments to its Asian allies, the seemingly ambivalent political aspirations of 12 million Taiwanese cannot be expected to merit lengthy and detailed discussion.

The validity of this third assumption has probably been questioned the least of the three assumptions up to this time. Apparently many people inside the U.S. Government—and more outside—still believe the Taiwanese are reasonably content with the government provided by the GRC. But it is the argument of this book that if a genuinely free election were held, following open and thorough debate, the people of Taiwan would vote the GRC out of office by a substantial majority and would establish an independent Taiwan.

It is also concluded here that the GRC is not the stable, firmly entrenched regime that U.S. policy makers have, at least well into the 1960s, assumed it to be. The Mainlanders, who appear confident of ultimate GRC success and are solidly united in their opposition to Taiwan autonomy, are, beneath the surface, far from confident of the stability of the GRC. In fact, they live with the constant realization that the GRC's days are numbered. Their ostensible confidence and solidarity in reality serve only to postpone the inevitable day of reckoning.

Since 1960, successive U.S. administrations have exhibited increasing doubts about the validity of the three assumptions upon which the China policy of this country was established in the 1950s. Yet the policy of support for Chiang Kai-shek's regime has continued into the 1970s.

What caused this inertia? Why did the China policy of the early 1950s continue for so long, even though it failed to reflect the realities of China and Taiwan as these realities were perceived by an ever increasing number of informed observers, both in and out of government? There was enough information available to provide policy makers with a reasonably accurate picture of China and Taiwan. The problem was that policy decisions were not fully responsive to this information. Instead, U.S. policy has been determined primarily in response to domestic political attitudes which, in regard to Taiwan and China, reflected the most undiscriminating Cold War anti-communism. Until the Vietnam War led the American people to realize the costs of unlimited opposition to communism and forced the United States to re-evaluate its position in Asia, domestic political pressures discouraged policy makers from publicly questioning the original assumptions behind China policy.

As for the academic community, whose role should be to shake the lethargy that forms once a policy becomes fixed, its spokesmen have been relatively vague and indecisive about the real situation in Taiwan. China scholars have with few exceptions viewed Taiwan as a side show; the center ring, for them, has been the Chinese mainland.

The few scholars who looked favorably upon the political aspirations of the Taiwanese, or who thought it dangerous for the United States to support a GRC claiming the right to overthrow the government in Peking, have long been unable to make themselves heard. They have had little chance to compete successfully against the vigorous anti-Peking and pro-Taipei views that, until recently, pervaded the U.S. Congress and were strongly supported by American public opinion. Scholars have been further hampered by lack of opportunity to conduct systematic political research on Taiwan, where open discussion of political questions can be grounds for expulsion of foreigners and imprisonment for their Taiwanese friends.

Today, U.S. China policy is in a state of flux. The United States, while trying to improve relations with Peking, has admitted rather explicitly that the GRC has no claim to speak for all of China. But is this enough? Can the United States establish reasonably normal relations with Communist China while continuing to support a regime on Taiwan that claims—even against the wishes of the United States—to be the legitimate government of all China? As American diplomats probe Peking for an answer to this question, they should not fail to explore the prospects that might open up if the people of Taiwan were given the opportunity to choose their own government.

If the Taiwanese were given self-determination, the United States would no longer have to contend with the salient contradiction inherent in the present policy—that of trying on the one hand to improve relations with China, and on the other of supporting a GRC that claims the right to overthrow the government in Peking.

Notes

1. Congressional Quarterly Service, *China and U.S. Far Eastern Policy 1945-1966* (Washington, D.C.: Congressional Quarterly, Inc., 1967), pp. 47-48. (Hereafter cited as CQ.)

2. *Department of State Bulletin (DSB),* January 16, 1950, p. 79.

3. On August 4, 1949, Acheson sent a memorandum to the National Security Council stating that the Communist conquest of Formosa seemed likely and could not be prevented by political and economic means alone. See Tang Tsou, *America's Failure in China, 1941-50* (Chicago: The University of Chicago Press, 1963), p. 527. (Hereafter cited as *Failure.*)

4. *DSB,* January 16, 1950, p. 80.

5. *Ibid.,* p. 81.

6. John W. Spanier, *The Truman-MacArthur Controversy and the Korean War* (Cambridge, Mass.: The Belknap Press, 1959), p. 54.

7. *CQ,* p. 48.

8. See the Hearings Before the Committee on Armed Services and the Committee on Foreign Relations, U.S. Senate, 82nd Congress, 1st Session, *Military Situation in the Far East* (Washington: Government Printing Office), v. 3, pp. 1667-1669.

9. Tsou, *Failure,* p. 523.

10. *Ibid.,* p. 524.

11. *CQ,* p. 49.

12. McGeorge Bundy (ed.), *The Pattern of Responsibility* (Boston: Houghton Mifflin Co., 1952), p. 264.

13. Acheson's defense perimeter statement was originally made to the Senate Foreign Relations Committee on January 10, 1950, and was repeated two days later in a speech before the National Press Club in Washington. (Bundy, *op. cit.,* p. 199.)

14. Some concern about Korea had been shown, however. A House Minority (Republican) Report in July 1949 strongly criticized the administration for withdrawing U.S. occupation forces from Korea at that time, and Republican Representative Walter Judd predicted that once we removed our troops the Communists would capture South Korea within a year. Ronald J. Caridi, *The Korean War and American Politics: The*

Republican Party as a Case Study (Philadelphia: Univ. of Pennsylvania Press, 1968, pp. 30-31.

15. Spanier, *op. cit.*, p. 58.

16. Tsou, *Failure*, p. 530.

17. *DSB*, July 3, 1950, p. 5.

18. Quoted in Gregory Clark, *In Fear of China* (Melbourne: Lansdowne Press, 1967), p. 76.

19. *DSB*, September 11, 1950, p. 412.

20. Spanier, *op. cit.*, p. 58.

21. *Ibid.*, p. 58.

22. Tsou, *Failure*, p. 533.

23. Among those advocating this position were Senators Knowland, Milliken, and Hickenlooper. Caridi, *op. cit.*, p. 123.

24. A. T. Steele, *The American People and China* (New York: McGraw-Hill Book Co., 1966), p. 47.

25. Truman's extensive account of the conversation is in his *Memoirs: Years of Trial and Hope* (New York: Doubleday and Co., 1956), pp. 398-410.

26. *Ibid.*, p. 403.

27. *The New York Times*, September 7, 1958, p. 3.

28. Truman, *op. cit.*, p. 407.

29. *Ibid.*, p. 410.

30. Truman's advisor, Averell Harriman, sounded out General MacArthur on this during a Far Eastern visit in August 1950, but MacArthur said he had seen no evidence of a desire for independence during his recent two-day visit to Formosa. Truman, *op. cit.*, pp. 352-353.

31. Department of State, *United States Relations with China* (Washington, D. C.: Government Printing Office, 1949), p. 309. (Hereafter cited as "White Paper.")

32. Spanier, *op. cit.*, p. 54.

33. "White Paper," p. 308.

34. George H. Kerr's *Formosa Betrayed* (Boston: Houghton Mifflin Co., 1965) is a useful source for critical information about Chiang's rule on Taiwan during the late 1940s. Most of this information would presumably have been available to concerned State Department officers, whether or not it reached the eyes of the president himself.

35. *CQ*, p. 12.

36. Robert Blum, *The United States and China in World Affairs* (New York: McGraw-Hill Book Co., 1966), p. 114.

37. *DSB*, May 28, 1951, p. 847.

38. Roger Hilsman, *To Move a Nation* (Garden City, N. Y.: Doubleday and Co., 1967) p. 297.

39. Steele, *op. cit.*, p. 209.

40. *Ibid.*, p. 208.

41. June 28, 1957, speech in San Francisco. *DSB*, July 15, 1957, p. 95. See also, for instance, his March 11, 1957, statement at a SEATO meeting in Canberra. *DSB*, April 1, 1957, p. 530.

42. *DSB*, September 8, 1950, p. 389.

43. *Ibid.*, p. 387.

44. *DSB,* March 11, 1957, p. 405.

45. *CQ,* p. 84.

46. Blum, *op. cit.,* pp. 111-112.

47. John Foster Dulles, *War or Peace* (New York: MacMillan Co., 1950), p. 190.

48. Caridi, *op. cit.,* p. 237.

49. Louis L. Gerson, *The American Secretaries of State and their Diplomacy, Volume XVII, John Foster Dulles* (New York: Cooper Square Publishers, Inc., 1967), pp. 211-213.

50. *Ibid.,* p. 202.

51. Dwight D. Eisenhower, *The White House Years,* in two volumes: *Mandate for Change, 1953-1956* (1963), and *Waging Peace, 1956-1961* (1965) (Garden City, N.Y.: Doubleday and Co.).

52. Eisenhower, *Mandate for Change,* pp. 470-471.

53. *Ibid.,* p. 474.

54. *Ibid.,* p. 475.

55. Sherman Adams, *Firsthand Report* (New York: Harper and Brothers, 1961), pp. 48-49.

56. Eisenhower, *Mandate for Change,* p. 469.

57. Eisenhower, *Waging Peace,* p. 293.

58. Tang Tsou, *The Embroilment Over Quemoy: Mao, Chiang, and Dulles* (Salt Lake City: Univ. of Utah Press, 1959), pp. 32-33. (Hereafter cited as *Embroilment.*)

59. Eisenhower, *Waging Peace,* pp. 293-294.

60. Tsou, *Embroilment,* p. 15.

61. Eisenhower, *Waging Peace,* p. 301.

62. *Ibid.,* p. 299.

63. Tsou, *Embroilment,* p. 18.

64. *Ibid.,* p. 18.

65. *Ibid.,* p. 41.

66. Eisenhower, *Mandate for Change,* p. 612.

67. *Ibid.,* p. 480. (This is Eisenhower's paraphrase of Dulles' answer.)

68. Eisenhower, *Waging Peace,* pp. 691-693.

69. *Ibid.,* p. 295.

70. *Ibid.,* p. 294.

71. Adams, *op. cit.,* pp. 127-128.

72. Robert J. Donovan, in *Eisenhower: The Inside Story* (New York: Harper and Brothers, 1956), says that after 1953, Eisenhower "was to speak out himself ever more forcefully against admission of Red China." (p. 136.)

73 Eisenhower, *Waging Peace,* p. 445.

74. *CQ,* p. 88.

75. Eisenhower, *Mandate for Change,* p. 612.

76. Quoted in Department of State Publication 6844, *The Republic of China* (October 1959), pp. 61-62.

77. *CQ, p.* 59.

78. Donovan, *op. cit.,* pp. 133-134.

79. Malcolm E. Jewell, *Senatorial Politics and Foreign Policy* (Lexington: Univ. of Kentucky Press, 1962), p. 64.

80. (Seattle: Univ. of Washington Press)

81. Pp. vii-viii.

82. P. 258.

83. Douglas Mendel, *The Politics of Formosan Nationalism* (Berkeley: Univ. of California Press, 1970), p. 41.

84. *Ibid.,* p. 41.

85. *Ibid.,* p. 5.

86. Rankin, *op. cit.,* p. 330.

87. Tang Tsou, *Failure,* p. 504, says that Robertson was "reportedly the choice of the leading members of the China block in Congress" for the assistant secretaryship. In Robertson's view the Peking government was "an outlaw-gangster regime, unpurged of its crimes and aggressions, and unfit to sit in any respectable family of nations." *DSB,* August 13, 1956, p. 264.

88. Eisenhower, *Mandate for Change,* p. 464.

89. In Hilsman's *To Move a Nation, op. cit.*

90. Theodore C. Sorensen, *Kennedy* (New York: Harper and Row, 1965).

91. Arthur M. Schlesinger, Jr., *A Thousand Days* (Boston: Houghton-Mifflin, 1965).

92. Kennedy readily admitted to Theodore H. White that his earlier charges had been "ignorant" and "wrong." *The Making of the President, 1964* (New York: Atheneum Publishers, 1965), p. 20.

93. However, Kennedy did not have a chance to vote for the proposed Lehman amendment, which would have clearly excluded the offshore islands, because he was at that time in the hospital recuperating from an operation.

94. Kennedy, *The Strategy of Peace* (New York: Harper and Brothers, 1960), p. 102.

95. *Ibid.,* pp. 103-104. (From a speech in September 1959.)

96. Hilsman, *op. cit.,* p. 319.

97. As the *CQ* review of Far Eastern policy, *op. cit.,* comments: "Return to the mainland has become the entire rationale for Chiang's leadership and the existence of his regime," p. 236.

98. Hilsman, *op. cit.,* p. 351.

99. *Public Papers of the Presidents of the United States: John F. Kennedy (1961)* (Washington: U.S. Government Printing Office, 1962), p. 546.

100. *Ibid.,* pp. 259-260.

101. Hilsman, *op. cit.,* p. 307.

102. *Ibid.,* p. 301.

103. *Ibid.,* p. 308.

104. Schlesinger, *op. cit.,* p. 483. Sorensen also records that Kennedy was "prepared to use whatever means were available to prevent the seating of Red China in Nationalist China's seat at the U.N." Sorensen, *op. cit.,* p. 665.

105. Hilsman, *op. cit.,* p. 318.

106. *Ibid.,* pp. 318-319.

107. Sorensen, *op. cit.,* pp. 661-662.

108. Hilsman, *op. cit.,* p. 319.

109. *CQ, op. cit.,* p. 236.

110. Hilsman, *op. cit.,* p. 310.

111. *CQ,* p. 236.

112. *Ibid.,* p. 236.

113. Hilsman, *op. cit.,* pp. 313-314.

114. *Ibid.,* pp. 311-312.

115. *Ibid.,* p. 314.

116. Sorensen, *op. cit.,* p. 662.

117. As the above-cited August 11, 1958, State Department statement of official U.S. policy pointed out, "Recognition of Communist China by the United States would seriously cripple, if not destroy altogether [the GRC]" *DSB,* September 8, 1958, p. 387.

118. Hilsman, *op. cit.,* p. 311.

119. *Public Papers of the Presidents of the United States: John F. Kennedy (1962)* (Washington: U.S. Government Printing Office, 1963), pp. 276-277.

120. Hilsman, *op. cit., p.* 298.

121. Holbert N. Carroll, "The Congress and National Security Policy," in David B. Truman (ed.) *The Congress and America's Future* (Englewood Cliffs, N. J.: Prentice Hall, Inc., 1965), p. 161.

122. Hilsman, *op. cit.,* p. 307.

123. *Ibid,.* p. 306. Hilsman says that the Mongolia move was, in fact, "indicative of a coming change in China policy," but gives no indication when it would be coming; it certainly was not imminent. Pp. 558-559.

124. *Ibid.,* p. 558.

125. *Ibid.,* p. 309.

126. According to Sorensen, *op. cit.,* p. 548, Kennedy told Khrushchev at their meeting in Vienna in June 1961 that withdrawal of American forces and support from Taiwan "would impair our strategic position in Asia." To this, Krushchev responded that if he were in Red China's position he would already have fought for Taiwan.

127. Sorensen, *op. cit.,* p. 755; Hilsman, *op. cit.,* p. 347.

128. *DSB,* May 11, 1969, p. 730.

129. Kenneth T. Young, *Negotiating with the Chinese Communists: The United States Experience, 1953-1967* (New York: McGraw-Hill Book Co., 1968), p. 329.

130. William S. White, *The Professional: Lyndon B. Johnson* (Boston: Houghton Mifflin Co., 1964), p. 242.

131. *DSB,* May 2, 1966, p. 694.

132. See Young, *op. cit.,* p. 231.

133. Quoted in Franz Schurmann and Orville Schell, *The China Reader: Communist China* (New York: Vintage Books, 1967), pp. 516-517.

134. *DSB,* August 1, 1966, p. 177.

135. *The New York Times,* October 8, 1960, p. 11.

136. *Ibid.,* p. 11.

137. *CQ, op. cit.,* p. 100.

138. *Ibid.,* p. 89.

139. *DSB,* September 1, 1969, p. 180.

140. *DSB,* February 17, 1969, p. 141.

141. *DSB,* December 1, 1969, p. 478.

142. *DSB,* December 4, 1970, pp. 733-735.

143. *DSB,* September 1, 1969, p. 180.

144. *The New York Times,* November 13, 1970, p. 4.

145. U.S. official spokesmen have compared the China/Taiwan situation with that of other divided countries such as Germany and Korea. If it is logical to recognize West Germany and South Korea as the legitimate governments of those countries then why not the GRC as the legitimate government of China? This argument can be made from a legal standpoint provided it is accepted that Taiwan is part of China. It is from the standpoint of political realities that it must be questioned. Few people other than Communist sympathizers will dispute that Bonn and Seoul are at least as qualified as Pankow or Pyongyang to speak for their respective peoples. The question in regard to China is a political one: Can Taipei really speak for and represent the interests of the 700-plus million people of mainland China?

146. This argument is made by the U.S. ambassador to the GRC, Walter McConnaughy, in the Hearings before the Subcommittee on United States Security Agreements and Commitments Abroad of the Committee on Foreign Relations, United States Senate, November 24, 25, and 26, 1969, and May 8, 1970, *United States Security Agreements and Commitments Abroad, Republic of China* (Washington: U.S. Government Printing Office, 1970), p. 942. (Hereafter cited as *U.S. Security Agreements.*)

147. This interpretation could logically be deduced from the testimony of Ambassador McConnaughy in *U.S. Security Agreements.*

148. One sometimes sees this argument presented by people in the State Department. Roger Hilsman, *op. cit.,* p. 346, tends toward this argument. He says China "clearly needed an outside enemy," and the United States was the ideal candidate.

149. *Peking Review,* November 26, 1965, p. 17. From November 19, 1965, editorial in the *People's Daily.*

150. Comments made to Canadian newsmen on June 29, 1961. *Peking Review,* July 14, 1961, p. 9.

151. Schurmann and Schell, *op. cit.,* p. 321.

152. Young, *op. cit.,* p. 317.

153. Young, *op. cit.*

154. *Ibid.,* p. 245.

155. U. Alexis Johnson also concluded, based on his experience as U.S. representative in the ambassadorial talks from 1953 to 1958, that Peking made Taiwan a stumbling block on every other issue. Young, *ibid.,* p. 319.

156. *Ibid.,* p. 292.

157. *DSB,* May 2, 1966, p. 688.

158. *The New York Times,* October 25, 1970, p. 29.

159. *Peking Review,* November 8, 1960, p. 22. When Chou said the United States sought to set up an "independent state" or a "Sino-Formosan

nation" he was obviously speculating about long-range U.S. motives and not commenting upon an actual U.S. proposal.

160. *Peking Review,* April 14, 1961, p. 6.

161. *Peking Review,* July 14, 1961, p. 9.

162. *Peking Review,* June 26, 1964, p. 6.

163. *CQ,* p. 209.

164. *Peking Review,* May 15, 1964, p. 8.

165. *Peking Review,* April 1, 1966, p. 14.

166. Edgar Snow, *Red Star Over China* (New York: Grove Press, 1968), p. 110.

167. *Ibid.,* p. 110.

168. A. Doak Barnett, *Communist China and Asia* (New York: Vintage Books, 1960), p. 408.

169. Schurmann and Schell, *op. cit.,* p. 325.

170. *DSB,* March 13, 1967, p. 423.

171. Some observers concerned with the Taiwan problem point to the experience of Tibet as an example of what might happen to Taiwan if the United States conceded that China had a legitimate interest in assuring that the settlement of the island's ultimate legal and political status not be determined without her consent. Once this right were granted, it is said, China would allow Taiwan no greater degree of genuine autonomy or self-determination than has been enjoyed in fact by Tibet, with its formal internal autonomy. But Taiwan's situation is very different from that of Tibet. Taiwan is separated from the mainland by 100 miles of water; it is relatively easily defensible and has a large, reasonably well-equipped army which should be an effective fighting force if under a leadership devoted to the defense of the island; furthermore, Taiwan will probably continue for some time to enjoy at least some degree of protection by the United States. This defensive capability would be a very strong bargaining point for the Taiwanese in working out the terms of their relationship with China. For the Chinese Communists, the conquest of a Taiwan united behind a popular government would be vastly more difficult than was the conquest of Tibet.

172. See the article "U.S. and Japanese Reactionaries Intensify Taiwan Independence Movement Scheme in Order to Perpetuate Their Occupation and Absorption of China's Sacred Territory of Taiwan." *People's Daily,* February 24, 1970. Reprinted in *T'ai-wan Ch'ing-nien,* March 1970, pp. 10-12.

173. As for academic interest, one view of Taiwan's value to the U.S. was offered by John K. Fairbank, perhaps the best known American student of Chinese history, who says: "We want contact with some part of [the] Chinese world that is friendly to us, that can be our window on Chinese life, a place to train our China specialists, a source of Chinese talent for us to train, a center for study of the mainland through Chinese eyes . . . ." *China: The People's Middle Kingdom and the U.S.A.* (Cambridge, Mass.: Belknap Press, 1967), p. 56.

174. This appears to be the conclusion, for instance, of U.S. Ambassador to the GRC Walter McConnaughy. See *U.S. Security Agreements, op. cit.*

175. At least four books published since 1964 have argued the case for the Taiwanese: *Formosa Betrayed,* by George Kerr (*op.cit.*); *The Politics of Formosan Nationalism,* by Douglas Mendel (*op. cit.*); *Formosa, China, and the United Nations,* by Lung-chu Chen and Harold Lasswell (New York: St. Martin's Press, 1967); and *Formosa Today,* edited by Mark Mancall (New York: Frederick A. Praeger, 1964).

176. Figures for both the National Assembly and the Legislative Yuan are for mid-1969. The December 1969 by-elections for new members of the National Assembly and the Legislative Yuan from Taiwan Province only slightly increased the percentage of Taiwanese representation in these bodies. These elections had no material effect on the issue of Taiwanese under-representation.

177. *The Independent Formosa,* Fall 1969, p. 10. Reprint of article by Fox Butterfield in *The New York Times,* October 12, 1969.

178. A review of Japanese rule is given in Mendel, *op. cit.,* pp. 16-25.

179. See, for instance, Mendel, *op. cit.,* p. 27.

180. The description of the early years of Nationalist rule in Mendel, pp. 26-41, and Kerr, throughout the book, were corroborated by numerous Taiwanese in conversations with this writer.

181. See, for instance, the above-quoted statement by General Wedemeyer in the "White Paper." Even the extremely pro-GRC Australian historian W. G. Goddard admits in *Formosa, A Study in Chinese History* (East Lansing: Michigan State Univ. Press, 1966), p. 178, that the behavior of the Nationalist administration "brought about public indignation and the subsequent uprising" (i.e., the February 1947 uprising).

182. The account that follows of the February incident and its aftermath it based largely on Kerr, *op. cit.,* pp. 232-330.

183. Not to be confused with Chinese Communist Foreign Minister Ch'en Yi.

184. See Mendel, *op. cit.,* p. 37; and Kerr, *op. cit.,* p. 310. A number of Taiwanese estimated "at least 10,000" in talking to this writer.

185. Kerr, *op. cit.,* p. 396.

186. Ch'en's activities in this regard are reported in Kerr, *op. cit.,* pp. 367-368. That Chiang only executed Ch'en after Ch'en contacted the Communists is common knowledge among both informed Mainlanders and informed Taiwanese on Taiwan.

187. *CQ,* p. 49.

188. *Free China Review,* May 1970, Vol. XX, No. 5, p. 16. In commenting on Chiang's trip, *The China News* (English language daily in Taipei) said: "Vice Premier Chiang also made it clear to both the American government and people that mainland liberation is attainable within the foreseeable future. Possibly the Americans will now be less likely to dismiss counterattack and mainland recovery as mere phrases for Taiwan domestic consumption." Quoted in *Free China Review,* May 1970, pp. 18-19.

189. *Ibid.,* p. 18.

190. *U.S. Security Agreements,* p. 943. According to Neil H. Jacoby in his thorough review of U.S. aid to Taiwan, "the dominant political effect of [U.S.] aid was to consolidate and stabilize the power of the Na-

tionalist government." *U.S. Aid to Taiwan* (New York: Frederick A. Praeger, 1966), p. 170.

191. Approximately 30% of the Taiwanese students abroad are believed to associate themselves actively with the TIM; this writer heard this figure mentioned by Taiwanese on Taiwan. Considering the fact that the GRC harasses the families of those that do and that those involved cannot safely return home for visits, this is a substantial percentage.

192. *The Independent Formosa,* Spring 1970, p. 12. *The China News,* on May 25, 1970, praised Chiang's speech and echoed his view that the "so-called Formosan independence movement is . . . merely a handful of Communist-inspired and misguided individuals who occasionally shout slogans and demonstrate." *Free China Review,* July 1970, p. 57.

193. This assessment of the views of the TIM abroad is based on two periodicals: *The Independent Formosa,* published by the World United Formosans For Independence (WUFI), in New York; and *T'ai-wan Ch'ing-nien* in Chinese, published by WUFI, in Tokyo.

194. Mendel, *op. cit.,* p. 49. The figure 90% was corroborated by Ambassador McConnaughy. See *U. S. Security Agreements, op. cit.,* p. 935.

195. Mendel, *op. cit.,* p. 118.

196. For a published account of the P'eng affair, see Mendel, *op. cit.,* pp. 117-118.

197. Mendel points out that shortly after Liao returned to Taiwan his brother, niece, and sister-in-law were released from prison and speculates that a GRC promise to Liao to release them might have been one of the factors causing Liao to return. *Op. cit.,* p. 151.

198. *The Independent Formosa,* Fall 1969, p. 2, has estimated editorially that there are "currently at least 30,000 political prisoners." Another estimate by a group of Taiwanese students was 8,000. *The Independent Formosa,* Spring 1969, p. 12.

199. See, for instance, Gregory Clark, *op. cit.,* p. 69.

200. Mancall, *op. cit.,* p. 32, footnote.

201. WUFI has denounced the attempted assassination, but has readily admitted that the attempted assassins were WUFI members. *The Independent Formosa,* Spring 1970, p. 5. WUFI was established on January 1, 1970, in order to unite TIM groups in the U.S., Japan, Europe, Canada, and, it claims, in Taiwan itself.

Definition of Terms

Taiwan:
Chinese name of Formosa. "Taiwan" is used in this book, although the two terms are often used interchangeably.

GRC:
Government of the Republic of China (i.e., the Nationalist Chinese Government presently on Taiwan).

KMT:
Kuomintang (the Chinese Nationalist Party), which holds a monopoly of meaningful political power on Taiwan.

Chinese:
In this book, refers to Chinese on the China mainland or to the People's Republic of China.

Mainlanders:
(Capitalized in this book.) Chinese who arrived in Taiwan after 1945, or their children born on Taiwan. Mainlanders occupy virtually all important policy-making positions in the GRC. Mainlanders constitute about 15 percent of the population of Taiwan.

Taiwanese:
Ethnic Chinese who were born on Taiwan before 1945 or whose forefathers were resident on Taiwan before 1945. Taiwanese are descended from immigrants from southern China, most of whom arrived in Taiwan in the seventeenth, eighteenth

and nineteenth centuries. Very few arrived after 1895, when Japan annexed Taiwan.

Native Taiwanese:

Same as "Taiwanese." In this book the term is not limited to the 170,000 or so aborigines, neither racially nor ethnically Chinese, who reside primarily in the mountains of eastern Taiwan. (GRC statements sometimes use the term "native Taiwanese" to describe the aborigines, while referring to the Taiwanese as "native-born" Chinese.)

Index